A SHORT HISTORY
OF DUBLIN

A SHORT HISTORY OF DUBLIN

RICHARD KILLEEN

Gill & Macmillan

Gill & Macmillan Ltd
Hume Avenue, Park West, Dublin 12
with associated companies throughout the world
www.gillmacmillan.ie

© Richard Killeen 2010
978 07171 4417 4

Index compiled by Cover to Cover
Typography design by Make Communication
Print origination by Carole Lynch
Printed in the UK by CPI Cox and Wyman, Reading

This book is typeset in Minion 11pt on 14pt.

5 4 3 2 1

*This book is for
Louisa*

CONTENTS

01 | RIVERRUN

Dublin wraps around a C-shaped bay, but it offers no natural deep-water harbour. The bay is shallow and tidal with a series of treacherous sandbars. None the less, the bay is the widest potential refuge for shipping on the east coast of Ireland. It is fed by a modest river, the Liffey, but one which is navigable at high water. It also commands the shortest sea crossing to Britain carrying shipping to north Wales and to the estuaries of the Mersey and the Dee, thus giving access to the rich middle and south of England.

In Roman times, the imperial outpost of Chester at the mouth of the Dee was the most significant port in north-west England. It is only a half-truth to state that the Romans never came to Ireland. There have been many archaeological finds of Roman coins and artefacts on the east coast, proof of commerce and intercourse between Roman Britain and the smaller island. The connection between Chester and Dublin endured for centuries. The patron saint of Chester in early Christian times, Werburgh, is commemorated in a prominent parish church in central Dublin, just a stone's throw from Christ Church Cathedral.

The mouth of the Liffey afforded easy access to the Irish midlands. Due west, there are few natural obstacles to the progress of immigrants, settlers and invaders. While the same might be said of the mouth of the River Boyne, about forty kilometres to the north—whose valley holds the richest evidence of prehistoric settlement on the island—the river itself offers no harbour or bay to compare with Dublin.

The only other location that might have challenged the Liffey was Waterford at the south-east corner of the island, with its magnificent three-river estuary offering shipping an unrivalled safe haven. However, its most direct cross-channel passage carried you to west Wales, a region of stubborn remoteness, impervious over the centuries to settlement by Romans, Vikings, Normans, the English and the rest of the world generally. Waterford was in time to develop into an important port, but it never offered a serious challenge to Dublin for overall primacy.

———

Dublin offered a series of advantages, therefore, which in aggregate made it the most plausible location for a significant east-coast settlement. The origins of the first settlers are long lost to history, but it appears that the landward side was as important as the seaward in this process. At Church Street Bridge, a natural ford allowed passage across the river at low tide. From this point, a series of ancient roads penetrated to the interior. The ford itself was prone to inundation at spring tides and storms, so a sturdier artificial ford was constructed slightly upstream. This was the Ford of the Hurdles or, in Irish, *Átha Cliath*, from which the modern city takes its name in that language: *Baile Átha Cliath*, the town of the ford of the hurdles. These fords were a necessity, for the business of crossing the river was fraught with hazard. Over 700 members of a military raiding party are recorded as having drowned in the attempt in the eighth century.

Modern Dubliners are accustomed to the embanked river being contained behind its quay walls from Heuston Station to the sea. The embanking of the river began in Viking times, as the town gradually became a centre of trade and commerce, but for centuries it was a haphazard process. In its natural state, the watercourse covered a much greater area than today. It is only possible to speculate on its exact course, but it can be reconstructed with reasonable confidence.

On the north bank, the probable course of the river seems to have roughly followed the modern boundary as far east as the present Capel Street bridge, before gradually spreading to cover what is now the lower reaches of O'Connell Street. On the south side, however, a much more dramatic effect was created in what is now Parliament Street, the southern end of Temple Bar and the City Hall area. Here, a huge pool delivered the waters of the Poddle, a tributary whose course was later to wrap itself around the southern and eastern walls of Dublin Castle, into the Liffey. All the modern streets and places just mentioned stand on land reclaimed from this triangular Poddle pool. The dark waters of this pool bore the Irish name *Dubh Linn*, which in time came to denote the whole district to the east of the Poddle confluence, while the area to the west retained the older name of *Átha Cliath*. The eastern settlement was principally the site of religious houses; the older, western one was mainly secular in purpose. Of the two Irish-language names, it was *Dubh Linn* that was eventually anglicised to give the city its name.

———

There was evidence of settlement around the bay from Mesolithic times, more so from the later Neolithic period. Still, this takes us back to about 4000 BCE. The Celts, who first irrupt into Ireland around 250 BCE, also appear to have had some sort of settlement on the rising ground above the ford close to Christ Church. This was the obvious location for a settlement, being contiguous to the ford—and therefore to the system of roads and trading routes—and defensible. This also became the focus of the Viking and Norman towns.

Ptolemy's map of the second century CE shows Ireland as a triangular island to the west of Britain, with a settlement about half way along the east coast called Eblana. This is the earliest cartographical acknowledgment of Dublin. There has been a great deal of scholarly dispute about this claim, but it seems that there was a settlement of sufficient significance in this region to come to the notice of Ptolemy in faraway Alexandria. On the logic of the discussion above, any such settlement was most likely to have been found around the shores of Dublin Bay.

Whatever its nature, the settlement never developed the sinews of a town in any sense that modern people could acknowledge. That had to await the arrival of the Vikings, with whom the history of the city proper may be said to begin.

02 | BEGINNINGS: THE VIKING TOWN

The term Viking refers to groups of Scandinavian people from two principal regions: the south and west coasts of Norway and the Jutland peninsula to the south across the Skagerrak. These people, in possession of their lands from ancient times, had originally migrated across the Great Northern Plain of Europe, which offered few natural obstacles to such migration.

Quite what impelled the Vikings to their sudden, violent and energetic expansion overseas from the eighth century CE is uncertain. There may have been population pressures, which would have been particularly severe in Norway with its rocky coastal valleys trapped and surrounded by impassable mountains on the landward side. The combination of limited and poor land together with the unforgiving northern climate would have made such habitats especially vulnerable to population growth, with any surplus population impelled to shift for itself. The gradual development of the proto-kingdoms of Norway and Denmark in the early Viking period may also have caused tribal groups alienated from the move towards centralised kingdoms to seek their fortunes elsewhere.

Whatever the reasons, the facts are incontrovertible. The Vikings developed the finest fleet of seafaring craft in contemporary Europe, which carried them to Britain and Ireland, north-west France, and as far east as Novgorod in Russia. The first Viking raid on Britain occurred in 789, but the most dramatic early assault was on the holy island and monastery of Lindisfarne in Northumbria.

Two years after Lindisfarne, in 795, the Vikings appeared for the first time off the Irish coast and attacked the wealthy monastery on Lambay Island, just north of Dublin Bay. They were raiding in search of loot and treasure and in this they were not alone, for native Irish raiders did not scruple to emulate their example. Undefended monasteries and their riches made tempting targets. For almost half a century, these Viking depredations continued, with the Norse the principal presence on the east and south coasts while the Danes pushed farther inland in their shallow-draughted longboats.

This so-called 'hit and run' period ended in 841 with the establishment of a proto-settlement, known as a *longphort*, on the banks of the Liffey. A *longphort* was a defensible enclosure for shipping which offered adequate berthage and easy access to the open sea. The establishment of the settlement marks the foundation date of the city of Dublin. The towns of Cork, Limerick, Wexford and Waterford, each of Viking foundation, followed before 900.

The *longphort* was not a town, although a town was to grow from it. Its purpose was to give shelter. Shelter suggested some degree of permanence, if only in the winter months. Permanence suggested continuity; the domestication of skills; trade and commerce. The Vikings had established secure control of the sea lanes all around the larger island of Britain, including staging posts in places like the Isle of Man. In 866 they established themselves in the old Roman city of York, from where they controlled the first Norse kingdom in the north of England. In short, Dublin became a link in a chain of Viking trading centres, joined by their secure control of the sea.

The Dublin *longphort* lasted until 902, when the native Irish drove the Vikings out. The Vikings did not win all their battles with the Irish. On the other hand, there is evidence of intermarriage and social intercourse from the earliest days, of linguistic confusion and melding, and of *ad hoc* military and other alliances, both formal and informal. It has been speculated that the expulsion of the Vikings in 902 only affected the military leadership and that domestic tradesmen and suchlike remained behind.

What is clear is that Viking power on the banks of the Liffey was broken until 917, when the leading families returned from their English exile. In England, where urban settlement and development was more advanced than in Ireland, they would have seen towns that were sophisticated by the standards of the age. They brought this knowledge back to Dublin. From this point on, it is customary to refer to the Viking city's *dún* phase, from the Gaelic word for fortification. No longer merely a *longphort*, the town now had a permanent stockade within which the community could find security. That security was not absolute: there were Gaelic incursions throughout the tenth century. The settlement was burned down in 936 but Norse power was subsequently reasserted and the little town rebuilt.

Throughout the tenth century, control remained for the most part in Viking hands, although there were interludes of Gaelic success and the town passed into Irish hands for at least one short period towards the end of the century. From Dublin, the Vikings were able to raid inland, but it was their commerce across the Irish Sea—by now a Viking lake—that gave the town its *raison d'être*.

The commerce of Viking Dublin entailed trade with the Isle of Man and with Viking centres in Britain such as York. The slave trade was a significant feature of both its imports and exports, which also included animal hides, wool and jewellery. The stability of commerce found expression in the development of the urban infrastructure. The ever-increasing pressure from the Irish kings and warlords from the 980s onward was a problem, but also provided an opportunity. For as long as the battle for control was inconclusive, provisional arrangements and compromises in the form of inter-marriage alliances gave the town an increasingly mixed ethnic character. This in turn led to linguistic ambiguity, as Norse and Gaelic borrowed from each other and a hybrid form developed.

However, the pressure from the Gaelic world was persistent and ultimately proved decisive. From around 1000 CE, Viking power in the town was fatally com-promised. In part, this was due to the rise of Brian Boru as a true high king of a united Gaelic polity, providing for the first time in the island's history a more or less central political and military authority. Even then, Brian's centralising impulse met with resistance from provincial sub-kings and their princely underlings. In order to deal with them, Brian was content to permit Viking Dublin a continuing degree of local autonomy. However, the king of Leinster, Máel Mórdha, outbid Brian with promises of autonomy to Dublin and succeeded in enlisting the support of the Viking ruler, Sitric Silkenbeard, in a provincial revolt against the power of the high king.

The issue was joined at Clontarf, on the north shores of Dublin Bay, on Good Friday 1014. The Dublin Norse and their Leinster allies were augmented by Viking troops from Britain, Norway, Denmark and the Isle of Man. Against them was ranged Brian's coalition, princi-pally comprising troops from Munster, Connacht and the midlands.

The Battle of Clontarf, one of the most famous fights

in Irish history, is a misnomer. It did not take place on land now occupied by the modern suburb of that name, but most likely to the west of it in the general area of modern Ballybough. In fact, the most plausible location for the main battle is in the general vicinity of Croke Park.

Brian won, although the battle cost him his life as well as those of his son and 15-year-old grandson. This is important given the context of the battle. It is usually celebrated as the moment that Ireland was rid of the Viking yoke. This is an exaggeration. Norse power was undoubtedly weakened: they had backed the losing side in a major battle. But Sitric remained the ruler of the town until his death in 1036. Vikings then retained the leadership of Dublin until at least 1042 and remained a significant presence until the arrival of the Normans over a century later. Even more significant was the failure of the Irish kings to deepen the centralising process that Brian had established in arms. His successors were unable to emulate him, leaving Gaelic Ireland politically divided and vulnerable to the next major invasion from a more sophisticated military society.

———

The effective assimilation of the Vikings was complete with their embrace of Christianity in the years after Clontarf. However, in a development that was to be hugely significant in the next century, they refused to accept the authority of the see of Armagh—the primatial Irish see—but placed themselves under the protection of Canterbury instead. This status was challenged at the Synod of Kells in 1152, which created the archdioceses of Dublin and Tuam to join the existing archepiscopal sees of Cashel and Armagh. It meant that the ecclesiastical status of Dublin was contested.

Christ Church Cathedral dates from 1038. It stood, as its successor stands today, on the southern lip of the ridge that rises from the river and along which ran the main thoroughfare of the town. Across the river, the church of St Michan dates from 1095 and formed the focus of a small suburban settlement. It was joined to the main town by a permanent bridge where Fr Mathew Bridge now stands. For 600 years, it remained the only parish church on the north bank of the river, but it became the focus of a series of religious settlements. A monastery dating from 1139 later became part of the Cistercian foundation known as St Mary's Abbey.

The most dramatic urban development of the so-called Hiberno-Norse period in the town's history—from 1014 to 1170—was the construction of the city walls. Hitherto, the various defensive enclosures and stockades had comprised earthen banks with timber reinforcements. But from the late eleventh century, the entire urban area was protected by a continuous stone wall, one of the very few contemporary towns in north-west Europe to be so defended. The walled area enclosed a space roughly bounded by Parliament Street, Essex Street East and Cook Street and then arcing back in a loop that embraced Christ Church but excluded the site of what would later be St Patrick's Cathedral. St Audeon's Arch and another small section of the Hiberno-Norse wall are still extant between Cornmarket and Cook Street.

In many respects, the history of the city has been its expansion beyond these walls. This happened gradually in all directions over time, but the key direction was east, towards the bay. Over centuries, the city's centre of gravity moved east from the Christ Church area towards College Green and O'Connell Street, especially in the Georgian period. It is a pattern that is being repeated in our own time by the development of the docklands.

A crucial moment in this eastward drift came in the 1160s with the foundation the Augustinian priory of All Hallows at a site called Hoggen Green, now College Green. The site of the priory, which was closed at the dissolution of the monasteries, is now occupied by Trinity College. The provision of green areas for commonage and grazing was an important part of the town's extramural development. Horses and cattle were required for draught purposes and as a source of food, so grazing areas were a crucial part of the town's supply chain of essentials. The best known modern green—St Stephen's Green—started life in a similar way.

There was also a westward expansion beyond the walls along the line of what is now Thomas Street and immediately north and south of it, from the river into what later became the Liberties. But this area was never fashionable, nor was it a centre of power. It remains one of the poorer parts of the modern city. Power and influence tended east, following the progressive development of the port—with its crucial trading function—towards the bay.

In the period immediately before the arrival of the Normans, Dublin is estimated to have had a fleet of over 200 trading ships, plying routes to distant continental and Scandinavian ports as well as to major towns in the west of England. Of these, Chester and Bristol were the most important. There was also an important ship-building yard in the town.

———

The next major development in the city's history was the product of an intrigue and a turbulent life. Diarmait Mac Murchada, the king of Leinster, abducted one Dervorgilla, the wife of a minor regional king called O'Rourke. Whether the lady consented to be abducted or not is unclear, but the upshot was that O'Rourke—understandably humiliated to be made a cuckold—appealed to Rory O'Connor, the king of Connacht and the provincial ruler with the nearest claim to call himself high king. O'Connor's muscle saw Mac Murchada lose his kingdom. He was forced to flee abroad.

Diarmait eventually found his way to the Norman king of England, Henry II, then on campaign in Aquitaine. Henry was sympathetic but could not spare any of his troops to help Diarmait recover his kingdom.

He did, however, however, give him letters authorising him to raise troops in Henry's lands back in Britain. In return, Diarmait pledged to hold Leinster as Henry's vassal and to offer his daughter's hand to whatever military leader might be found in Henry's lands.

This possibility immediately secured a potential interest for the crown of England in the island of Ireland. There was already the uncertain ecclesiastical loyalty of the see of Dublin to confuse the issue, not to mention a papal bull of 1155, *Laudabiliter*, which authorised Henry II to invade Ireland in order to enforce religious conformity. This bull was almost certainly prompted by the see of Canterbury—nettled by the 'transfer' of Dublin to Armagh's jurisdiction under the terms of the Synod of Kells. Moreover, Canterbury would have had a ready ear in Pope Adrian IV (Nicholas Breakspear, the only Englishman ever to hold the office). The net effect was that Henry II had a papal warrant to invade Ireland should it suit him. It did not, but he had no objection to helping Diarmait recover his kingdom.

And so it was done. Diarmait raised troops in Wales, returned and recovered some of his lands in 1167, and was reinforced by more Norman troops that landed in 1169 and an even more formidable force in 1170. Its leader was Richard fitzGilbert, deposed Earl of Pembroke, known to history as Strongbow. It was he who claimed the hand of Diarmait's daughter Aoife.

Strongbow and his men captured Dublin in that same year. The Anglo-Norman era had begun.

03 | THE NORMAN CITY

The Normans had originally been a Viking tribe that established itself in north-west France in the tenth century. Over time they became thoroughly assimilated in their new land and from about 1000 CE we can speak of them as French. They then emerged as one of the most remarkable expansive forces in medieval Europe. They sent bands of adventurers into the Italian peninsula. By 1130, they had ousted the Saracens and established a kingdom in southern Italy and Sicily, which over time was to mutate into the famous Kingdom of the Two Sicilies. They were the leading force in the establishment of the Christian kingdom in Palestine in 1099 following the First Crusade.

To the north, they conquered England in 1066. The Norman Conquest wrought the destruction of Anglo-

Saxon England and transformed the country. Just over a century later, their knights under Strongbow were in Ireland.

They captured Dublin and resisted an attempt by Rory O'Connor, the *soi-disant* high king, to take the city. Diarmait Mac Murchada died in his hour of triumph, leaving Strongbow as lord of Dublin and much of eastern Ireland. Word of all this reached Henry II, who, fearing that Strongbow could use his Irish base to recover his lost earldom of Pembroke or—worse—set up a separate lordship in Ireland, came to Ireland, made a show of force, and secured the loyalty of Strongbow and Dublin and the submission of many Irish chiefs.

Dublin now ceased to be an independent city state but instead became a dependency of the crown of England. But England in turn was in the power of foreign French-speaking *conquisadores*. French was the language of law and power and the country's interests were thoroughly aligned with France, where King Henry II was, through inheritance and marriage alliances, effective ruler of the western one-third of the country.

All this introduced Dublin to the usages of continental urban government and its representative institutions. The key document in this process was the royal charter. This was a grant of lands and privileges from the crown. The grant was usually made in perpetuity, thus giving legal certainty. Henry granted Dublin to the freemen of Bristol, extending to them privileges similar to those that they enjoyed back home. Of these, the most important were the right to trade free of tolls and customs duties. The granting of the charter gave Dublin a legal personality in English medieval law. It was the authoritative and uncontested source of municipal legitimacy for the Norman town. As such, it emphasised the unique authority of the king as the sole source entitled to grant such a charter of rights.

We may now begin to use the word city rather than town, because while the population and extent of twelfth-century Dublin hardly merits the term, the granting of the charter does. The definition of a city in the Anglo-Norman tradition was a place held by royal charter or enjoying cathedral status. Indeed, the Normans placed even greater emphasis than before on religious foundations. The number of secular parishes increased, as did the number of monastic establish-ments. These were rich foundations, generously endowed, and they played an important role in charity works as well as in the physical development of the city outside the walls. As major landowners, they had a corporate interest in what we would now call property development. They were run by worldly men, not simply the pious contemplatives of caricature.

Of the ecclesiastical structures outside the walls, the most important was the church of St Patrick, which was built by Archbishop John Comyn and dedicated in 1192. Built on the site of a Patrician well on what was then an island in the River Poddle, it was raised to cathedral status in 1213 by Archbishop Henry de Londres following a dispute with Christ Church. Thus there now stood two cathedrals within a kilometre of each other, one inside the walls and one without. They still stand today, although hardly any of the fabric of the original buildings remains—both were the innocent victims of well-intentioned but clumsy Victorian restoration—and the wall between them, of course, has completely disappeared. St Patrick's is the national cathedral of the Church of Ireland, Christ Church the diocesan cathedral of the archdiocese of Dublin.

————

Henry II's charter of 1171 was the beginning of a process. Twenty years later, King John issued a further charter. By 1229, municipal self-government had developed to the point that the city had its first elected mayor and council, which met in the Tholsel or town hall. Dublin's Tholsel stood opposite Christ Church Cathedral on a street called Skinner's Row, now Christchurch Place. The original medieval building was replaced in 1676 by a handsome arcaded structure that survived until it was demolished in 1791. By then, the city was in its Georgian pomp and its corporators felt that they had outgrown a building that they regarded as archaic and which was, in truth, in a dangerous state of disrepair. The corporation worthies then removed to the City Assembly Rooms in South William Street—now the Dublin Civic Museum—before finally taking over the magnificent Royal Exchange in 1852 and reconstituting it as the City Hall. It retains that role today.

Once the Normans were established, there was only one serious attempt made to overturn their settlement. In 1175, Rory O'Connor laid siege to the city and failed. Thereafter it stood secure. The walls were augmented and strengthened. Dublin Castle was built in the early thirteenth century, standing astride the ridge on the rising ground just south of the river. It remained the centre and symbol of English royal power in Dublin until 1922.

The granting of the charter to the men of Bristol emphasised an enduring feature of the city's life. Dublin faced both ways, towards the sea and towards the Irish hinterland to its rear. Of the two, the sea was the more important. The Viking town had formed as a maritime *entrepôt* and manufacturing centre. It retained these essential functions in medieval times, symbolised by the link to Bristol. This link also gave the city the air of an English redoubt, with its back turned to the Gaelic hinterland. Many maritime cities have this quality: London itself, New York, Sydney, Istanbul—places whose municipal self-possession leaves them relatively indifferent to the country behind. For much of its history, it makes better sense to see Dublin not as the principal city on the island of Ireland but as a colonial city state. After the Reformation, Dublin remained a Protestant city on a Catholic island until the nineteenth century.

The lifeblood of Norman Dublin was trade and manufacture. That meant the introduction of the guild system to the city. Merchant or trade guilds were associations formed by the practitioners of various avocations for mutual protection and the maintenance of standards. They combined the functions of primitive trade unions and producers' monopolies. Unless a person held membership of the relevant guild, he could not practise the trade concerned. Membership of the early Dublin guilds was confined to 'persons of English name and blood', thus further emphasising ethnic exclusivity. This latter prescription was flexibly interpreted, because the Dublin guild merchant roll listed members not just of English provenance but from continental Europe as well. But the bottom line was: no Gaels.

In all, there were 25 Dublin guilds, each of which had representation on the city corporation. The municipal privileges attaching to guild membership lasted until the passage of the Municipal Corporations Act 1840, which went a long way towards democratising urban government. But for six centuries, the trade and merchant guilds were an essential element in the city government.

Early Norman Dublin boomed economically. The population grew rapidly and by the first half of the thirteenth century more than half the inhabitants lived outside the walls. The city pushed west towards Kilmainham, north into Oxmantown and south towards St Patrick's. Some suburban areas without the walls were denominated as Liberties, that is palatinate jurisdictions under the rule of local magnates to whom specific privileges were granted. These privileges

included the administration of justice and other functions normally exercised by the municipal authorities.
There were a number of such Liberties in the early
Dublin suburbs, of which the most prominent were
those of St Sepulchre—granted to the Archbishop—and
of St Thomas Court and Donore, which belonged to the
abbey of St Thomas. Indeed, the suburbs themselves
tended to cluster around powerful religious foundations.

After the dissolution of the monasteries in 1539, the
Liberty of St Thomas Court and Donore was transferred
to William Brabazon, whose descendants were to
become the Earls of Meath. Thus this area became
known in time as the Earl of Meath's Liberties. Today it
is simply called the Liberties. Perhaps the vitality of
medieval Dublin's growth can be conveyed by one of the
principal streets in the Liberties, New Street. It dates
from the thirteenth century.

On the riverfront, the gradual process of embanking
the river to create a deeper channel for merchant
shipping went on apace. Indeed, this was to be a constant in the city's life, for not only did the river need to
be contained but the sandbars in the bay remained a
menace to shipping for centuries. The river also needed
to be crossed, especially to give access to Oxmantown
and St Mary's Abbey. The ancient *Átha Cliath* and the
various structures that had superseded it were replaced
by a stone bridge, the first in the city's history, in 1215. It
remained the only river crossing until the seventeenth
century. Stone houses began to appear as well, whereas
the Viking town had comprised post and wattle

dwellings only. Of course, stone construction was a luxury for the rich. Yet the surviving remains of domestic stone construction are further evidence of economic growth.

Then came the disastrous fourteenth century. In 1315, Edward Bruce, brother of Robert the Bruce, victor of Bannockburn and king of Scotland, led an invasion force to Ireland. Edward was heir presumptive to his brother but he now proceeded to style himself king of Ireland. In this ambition, he had the support of at least some northern Gaelic chiefs. He landed at Larne in May 1315 and began an erratic three-year campaign, which was to end with his defeat and death at Faughart, near Dundalk. In February 1317 he presented himself in the western approaches to the city—in the region of modern Castleknock—with the clear intention of capturing it.

The response was decisive, ruthless and perhaps a bit panicky. To block his approach, the walls were strengthened and the suburbs burned. This was no small undertaking. The suburbs were more populous than the compact walled centre. They generated more tax revenue for the municipal authority. The retreat of such a number of citizens into the already crowded walled city must have created all the pressures that one can readily imagine in a medieval siege. Sanitation alone would have been a nightmare. The fact that the Bruce campaign in Ireland coincided with a three-year famine which is estimated to have killed one in 10 of the population of north-west Europe compounded the misery.

But the great fire did the job in the short run. Bruce hesitated. And as he did, an English force under Mortimer landed at Youghal and began to push towards Dublin. Bruce decided not to besiege the city. Instead he withdrew, to continue what remained of his incoherent campaign. The city had saved itself, but at a terrible price. Much of its physical expansion over the course of the preceding century was destroyed in the great fire. Within a generation, as it struggled to rebuild, an even greater disaster struck.

The Black Death—bubonic plague—was the most fearsome pandemic in European history. In less than a year, it spread from the Crimea, where it first announced itself, to every corner of the continent. It is estimated to have killed about a quarter of the total population of Europe—perhaps as many as 25 million people—although its effects were generally more lethal in the Mediterranean lands than in the north and west. Still, casualty rates in England are estimated at about 20 per cent of the entire population and there is little reason to doubt that the Irish figure was very different.

The Black Death reached Dublin in August 1348. In a malignant example of medieval globalisation, it had taken barely a year to travel the trade routes from one end of Europe to the other. By Christmas that year, it is estimated to have killed 14,000 people in the city.

04 | THE LONG MEDIEVAL DECLINE

The first Irish parliament had met at Castledermot, Co. Kildare, in 1264. It was a body composed exclusively of Hiberno-Norman magnates and its deliberations represented the concerns and anxieties of the colony, which was gradually contracting. For most of the thirteenth century, it had prospered and grown. But in the last quarter, from about 1275, the tide turned.

The whole colonisation process seemed to go into reverse. Gaelicisation took its place. The colonists were, so to speak, going native. Moreover, the natives themselves offered increasing resistance as the thirteenth century wore on. Lands previously yielded up were regained. Intermarriage and the adoption of Gaelic language and customs diluted the blood of the colony. A whole series of parliamentary statutes tried in vain to arrest this process. The most famous of these were the Statutes of Kilkenny (1366), which outlawed inter-marriage and the use of the Gaelic language, while insisting on the use of Common Law rather than the Gaelic Brehon Law. Like other similar statutes, they were largely ignored.

The process was relentless. By the late fifteenth century, only a small area around Dublin was securely under the direct control of the English crown. This was the famous Pale, an area running from the foothills of the mountains south of the city westward around the towns of Maynooth and Trim before curving back east to rejoin the sea at the fortified town of Dundalk.

The Pale was a fortified defensive border marking the outer limit of that territory where the king's writ ran. It was elastic, contracting more often than expanding as the fifteenth century wore on.

Beyond the Pale, one found what were in effect palatinate lands held by Hiberno-Norman magnates such as the earls of Kildare, Ormond and Desmond, or lands still in Gaelic ownership. For Dublin, this period confirmed its status as a provincial link in the Anglo-Welsh maritime world, ever more cut off from the greater Irish hinterland. It seemed that its glory days were behind it. The triple blow of famine, the great fire and the Black Death had enfeebled the urban fabric. The stone bridge had been dismantled in 1316 in order to reinforce the walls in the face of the Bruce threat. It was rebuilt, only to collapse in 1385 and not to be rebuilt again until 1428.

The fifteenth century continued the decline. No great public buildings were constructed. There were no developments in city government, nor any expansion of trade and commerce. Dublin hunched rather nervously behind the shelter of the Pale, a stagnant English trading colony. There were no additions made to the riverfront embankments between 1300 and 1500. The existing system of quays was insufficient to narrow the river channel and the older defences were in poor repair. This compounded the perennial problem of the sandbars in the bay. The result was that larger ships had to use Dalkey Sound for anchorage, with cargoes then being transported into the city by draught animals. Passenger ships usually berthed at Ringsend.

For most of the medieval period, the lordship of Ireland enjoyed a form of devolution under the leadership of a lord deputy sent over by the king. From about 1470 on, the position of lord deputy passed into the hands of the house of Kildare, which held it in more or less unbroken hereditary succession until the 1530s. This was a normal arrangement in composite royal states until relatively recent historical time. Difficulties of distance and communication and the absence of modern bureaucracies and centralised tax-gathering systems ensured that such practical devolution of power to the regions and the marchlands made sense. In effect, great magnates like the Kildares exercised palatinate powers.

This was the arrangement that was finally challenged and overthrown by the turbulent events of the 1530s. Two forces coalesced to produce what was a revolution from above. First, there was a new theory of kingship abroad in Europe, with a movement towards enhanced royal authority in a centralised royal state. This meant unitary kingdoms and the weakening of regional magnate power. Henry VIII wanted to move his kingdom in this direction. This meant clipping the wings of great magnate palatines such as the Percys in Northumberland and the Kildares in Ireland.

At the same time, he came to assert his independence in ecclesiastical matters. This was more a question of dynastic necessity than of ideology. His queen, Catherine of Aragon, had suffered a series of miscarriages and had only given birth to one surviving daughter, the future Queen Mary, in 1516. He wished to divorce her and marry the younger (and hopefully more fruitful) Anne Boleyn. Henry had good reason to fret over the succession. The memory of the chaotic Wars of the Roses was a recent one. The birth of a healthy male heir was essential to the security of the Tudor dynasty.

Henry petitioned the pope for a divorce, which was refused. The consequence was the break with Rome and the establishment of the royal supremacy in the years 1533–6. Thus was born the Church of England, with the Church of Ireland following suit in 1537. Although this was not a theological break—Henry died still believing himself a Catholic—it laid the indispensable foundation for the Reformation in both islands.

The royal supremacy in the church was all of a piece with the drive towards the centralising royal state. In Ireland, the earl of Kildare began to feel the heat. As early as 1519, he had first been summoned to court by Henry to give an account of himself, not being re-appointed lord deputy until 1524. In 1530, he was nominally replaced by Sir William Skeffington, but Kildare was still the real power in Ireland. In ack-nowledgment of this Kildare was reappointed in 1532. In 1534, however—the year that Henry was excommuni-cated by Rome—Kildare was once more summoned to London.

Henry's chief minister, Thomas Cromwell, was already intriguing against the Kildare interest and had allies in the Irish Council in Dublin. Kildare left his son Thomas, Lord Offaly, in charge back home with instructions to be wary of the Irish Council and to ignore any instruction to go to London. Offaly, better known to history as Silken Thomas, was able to maintain contact with his father. Kildare gave him regular advice, although also informing him that he had been forbidden to return to Ireland. In the meantime, the summons to London duly arrived and with it the belief on Thomas's part that his father had been disempowered by Henry.

What followed was the famous revolt of Silken Thomas. In association with his advisers and the traditional network of Kildare allies, he was attempting to demonstrate that Ireland could not be ruled without the co-operation and support of the traditional Kildare power base. Still, his defiance of the king went beyond anything that the Kildare faction had ever attempted previously.

On 11 June 1534, Silken Thomas and a retinue of over

100 horsemen burst in upon a meeting of the Irish Council in St Mary's Abbey. He resigned as vice-deputy, handing over the ceremonial sword of office to the lord chancellor. He then withdrew to Oxmantown, where he had troops billeted. This action was taken on the direct advice of his father and with the support of his advisers in Ireland. When word of this action reached London, Kildare was promptly clapped in the Tower, where he died—the exact circumstances are unknown—in September.

What made the rebellion of Silken Thomas different was the religious issue. Thomas denounced Henry as an apostate and called for allegiance to pope and emperor, to whom he sent emissaries soliciting aid for his cause. He also called for the expulsion of all Englishmen from the lordship of Ireland. This led to the capture of the archbishop of Dublin, John Alen, who was indeed English and who was duly murdered.

This was a direct challenge to the Henrician settlement in both church and state. Henry sent Skeffington to Ireland with a substantial army and with formidable artillery. The result was the total defeat of Silken Thomas and the destruction of Kildare power for ever. Their hitherto impregnable castle at Maynooth fell to the royal guns. Silken Thomas and five of his uncles were shipped to London and executed. The Kildare power was broken and their vast land holding forfeit to the crown. It was the end of the Middle Ages.

The effect of all this on Dublin was twofold. First, it raised the status of the city from a trading outpost to a centre of royal government. Henry's determination to transform the way in which Ireland was governed was symbolised in 1541 by the creation of the kingdom of Ireland. No longer a mere lordship, it was henceforth to be a sister kingdom. Dublin was now a royal capital, albeit a rather shabby one. More immediately dramatic in its effect on the city's fabric was the dissolution of the monasteries.

The city was rich in religious foundations. As we noted earlier, suburban development tended to cluster around religious houses, which were frequently impressive structures within walled enclosures. It is estimated that 20 per cent of all land in the city, its suburbs and the surrounding county was owned by religious houses. The disappearance of such a large body of long-established institutions had a dramatic effect. All but one of the Dublin monasteries that were suppressed were located in the suburbs, outside the city walls. The most significant of these in later history was the Augustinian Priory of All Hallows, which stood in the far eastern suburbs on a site just south of the river as it opened towards the bay.

All Hallows was suppressed in 1538, the canons were pensioned off and the site was granted to Dublin Corporation in thanks and compensation for the physical damage the city had sustained during the Silken Thomas rebellion. The site was neglected by the Corporation. It was used as a temporary pest house during a plague outbreak in the 1570s but it was not properly developed until 1592, when the long-awaited university was established on the site in Queen Elizabeth 1's reign. Nothing survives of the original buildings in Trinity. The oldest buildings in the modern university are the Rubrics, between Library Square and New Square.

Near the suppressed foundation of All Hallows, the convent of St Mary de Hogges suffered a similar fate, the property passing through a number of hands before becoming the property of Sir Arthur Chichester, the lord deputy, in 1604. Chichester House was used as the home of the Irish parliament on and off during the seventeenth century before falling into a state of disrepair and being demolished in 1728. The foundation stone of the replacement Parliament House was laid in the following year and the magnificent new building—known to us as the Bank of Ireland, College Green—was opened in 1733.

Many other religious houses suppressed in the late 1530s survive vestigially in the city's street names. Thomas Street, Francis Street, John's Lane, Andrew Street, Peter Street and Nicholas Street all take their names from the patron saints of dissolved religious houses. Mary Street recalls St Mary's Abbey, the oldest and richest foundation on the north side. Dame Street, built to connect the Castle to Trinity, takes its name from the church of St Mary del Dam which stood just inside the city walls between where Sycamore Street and Crane Lane now stand.

The long reign of Elizabeth I (1558–1603) saw the secure establishment of Protestantism in Britain but not in Ireland. The Irish elite remained Catholic, Old English (as we shall refer to the Hiberno-Normans from here on) and Gaelic chiefs alike. The allegiance of the elites was key, for in an age of deference it determined the allegiance of the common people. The shared recusancy of the 'two nations' gave them a common cause, although it required many more generations before the old ethnic suspicions between Gael and Old English were to disappear.

The term Old English is used to distinguish long-established families of Norman origin from the New English, a very different breed. The New English were the administrators, planters, soldiers and adventurers who came to Ireland in the years following the Henrician reforms. They were Protestants to a man. The whole history of Ireland in the sixteenth century is the crown's attempt to make its writ run throughout Ireland and to reverse the Gaelic revival of the late medieval period that had seen the Pale shrink so badly. This was an enterprise that brought limited success, with plantations in Munster and the midlands following the defeat and dispossession of Old English magnates and Gaelic chiefs alike. The culmination of this process was the Nine Years' War, which brought an end to the hitherto impregnable and undefeated world of the Ulster Gaelic lords.

Elizabeth was succeeded in 1603 by James I, whose Irish administration was firmly in the hands of aggressive New English like Chichester and Sir John Davies, the attorney-general. From Dublin Castle, they issued proclamations against religious tolerance—calling for public conformity to the Church of Ireland

and attendance at Divine Service—and so harried the defeated Gaelic lords of Ulster that they fled abroad: the famous Flight of the Earls.

The first map of the city of Dublin appeared in 1610. Speed's Map, so called for its maker, is an iconic document. It shows what is still in essence the medieval city. The two and a half centuries since the Black Death had seen no sustained recovery either in commerce or population. Plagues still ravaged the city from time to time. Compared to the vitality and optimism of the thirteenth century, it seemed a paltry legacy. The population was probably no more than 15,000 persons (and Speed's map could be interpreted to yield a lower figure), a poor comparison with the estimate for the late thirteenth century (35,000).

The turbulent politics of the 1640s were crucial in the making of modern Ireland. The rebellion of 1641 was principally an attempt to reverse the Plantation of Ulster, which had seen Anglo-Scots settlers take over the lands of the Gaelic earls who had fled. The conspirators plotted to capture Dublin Castle, were betrayed by careless talk and found themselves not in possession of the castle but incarcerated in it. Then Gaelic lords and the Old English made common cause in the Catholic interest. But that interest was ultimately dependent on the good will of the English crown, which under King Charles I was inclined towards religious tolerance—or at least what passed for it in an age of violent religious controversy. Charles lost the English civil war to his parliamentary opponents, who promptly executed him.

They were robustly Protestant and it was their military commander, Oliver Cromwell, who landed at Ringsend on 15 August 1649, bent on revenge for Catholic atrocities committed during the failed 1641 rebellion.

By the time he left Ireland less than a year later, he was well on the way to achieving what no English ruler since 1170 had managed: the effective subjugation of the entire island and the projection of English law and power into every corner of the land. His regime in England barely survived his death in 1658. Two years later, Charles II, son of the executed king, arrived home from exile in France and resumed the throne as king of England, Scotland and Ireland. To Ireland, he sent as viceroy or lord lieutenant his father's old associate, James, Duke of Ormond, successor to the great medieval Butler dynasty. The duke arrived in Dublin on 27 July 1662, on which date the history of the modern city may be said to begin.

05 | ORMOND AND THE NEW DUBLIN

The country that the Duke of Ormond inherited had been transformed by Oliver Cromwell, who, in the famous phrase, had 'like a lightning passed through the land'. His direct effect on Dublin was minimal. He stabled his horses in St Patrick's Cathedral, but apart from inflicting that indignity he left no lasting physical imprint on the city.

However, he changed the entire context of the city's life. By dispossessing the vast majority of Catholic land-owners in the provinces of Leinster and Munster and settling the lands on New English landlords, he put in place a colonial ruling class. Land ownership meant political and economic power in the pre-industrial age. The dispossession of the old elite—Old English and Gaelic alike, Catholics to a man, and all of them come of families established in Ireland for centuries—to be replaced by a new Protestant gentry was meant to secure Ireland for the English interest and for the Reformation. It was a revolution.

It meant that three of the four Irish provinces—the poorest, Connacht, being the exception—were now firmly in New English and Protestant hands. Cromwell had made no distinctions on ethnic grounds. To him, Old English and Gaels were all Catholics and were equally complicit in the outrages committed in the 1641 rebellion. This is an important moment in Irish history, when the sheer pressure of a revolution from above creates a new consciousness, substituting religious solidarity for ethnic identity as the key variable. After Cromwell, a sense of shared Catholic solidarity and grievance replaces the older distinction between the 'two nations' of medieval Ireland. Besides, both had a different kind of 'new nation' to live with, in the shape of the parvenu landlords.

The Duke of Ormond faced a delicate task. The restoration of the monarchy had raised hopes among the dispossessed that the Cromwellian land settlement would be overturned or at least gravely weakened. It soon became clear that neither Ormond nor the king felt willing or able to satisfy these hopes. The new regime was neither strong enough nor secure enough to satisfy such demands. The pattern of land ownership established by Cromwell was to endure until the Land Acts of the late nineteenth and early twentieth centuries broke up the estates and established the former tenants as proprietors.

Ormond's Dublin was beginning to acquire some of the sinews of the modern city. From the early seventeenth century, it had become the sole seat of the Irish parliament. The medieval parliament had been peripatetic, meeting as often in Drogheda or Kilkenny as in Dublin. The century also brought the gradual return of economic growth. Dublin began to expand again, with notable suburban development on the north bank of the Liffey and to the west of the walled city towards Kilmainham. A city that had only ever had one bridge (and, as we saw, not even that for a time in the late Middle Ages) acquired four more between 1670 and 1683. Three of these bridges still exist, although all have been reconstructed over time.

The finest of these new bridges was on the site of the modern Capel Street Bridge and represented a further shift of the city's centre of gravity eastward towards the bay. It created a new north–south axis from the Castle and made the development of the northern suburbs beyond a tempting prospect. This is exactly what happened in the great eighteenth-century building boom, with the earliest fashionable Georgian developments located north of the river.

Perhaps the most enduring legacy bequeathed the city by the Duke of Ormond is the Phoenix Park. On his arrival in 1662, he took up residence in the Phoenix Manor, which stood on the site of the modern Magazine Fort. He acquired 2,000 acres around the manor as a viceregal deer park. One of the previous owners from whom he bought the land was Sir Maurice Eustace, the speaker of the Irish House of Commons, whose name lives on in a street in Temple Bar. The duke stocked the park with deer, whose descendants are still to be seen there today.

Another notable Ormond legacy is St Stephen's Green. This had existed from medieval times as a pasture area for cattle and horses in the distant south-east reaches of the small town. By 1664, when its 27 acres were denominated by the Dublin Corporation as a public leisure area, it was still distant from the city centre. Building lots were sold to enclose the green and were gradually developed for town houses. There was a problem, however. The route linking Trinity College and the Green was deemed to be 'so foule and out of repair that persons cannot pass to the said Green for the benefit of the walks therein'. Something had to be done and in 1671 the Corporation set about the improvements that in time led to the development of Grafton Street.

Grafton Street in its modern form dates from 1708 and was named for Charles Fitzroy, 2nd Duke of Grafton, who was the lord lieutenant at the time. He was a grandson of King Charles II: his father, Henry Fitzroy, was (as the surname suggests) the illegitimate son of the king and Barbara Villiers, Duchess of Cleveland, the most beautiful and notorious of the king's many mistresses.

The 1680s brought a building boom to Dublin. Churches were built or rebuilt. Francis Place's panoramic drawing of the city in 1698 shows 17 church towers and spires, giving the cityscape a vertical definition that it had previously lacked. The Liberties became increasingly populated and densely housed. This area also became the centre of Huguenot life in the city. The Huguenots were French Protestants, a community of religious dissenters whose position in France deteriorated throughout the seventeenth century. The French wars of religion in the previous century had been a national disaster and Louis XIV was determined to enforce religious uniformity in the country. This made life increasingly difficult for non-Catholics and so, from the 1660s on, there was a steady stream of Huguenot emigrants to Protestant cities like London and Dublin.

Like many talented exiles, they contributed to their host societies in a manner out of all proportion to their numbers. They were skilled craftsmen, especially talented at textile weaving and silk production. Their industry encouraged the development of these trades in Dublin; the name Weaver's Street in the modern Liberties is a reminder of their presence. Huguenot numbers grew hugely after the Revocation of the Edict of Nantes in 1685. This edict, which had been in place in France since 1598, had allowed for a degree of religious tolerance, but it was offensive to Louis XIV's desire for religious uniformity. Louis' policies were to find an ironic echo in Ireland in the eighteenth-century penal laws, enacted for a similar purpose in a Protestant milieu.

Most of the 1680s was consumed in the construction of the greatest civic building in seventeenth-century Dublin, and the first one in the city that was unambiguously post-Renaissance in design. The Royal Hospital at Kilmainham was built as a residence for homeless ex-soldiers. The model—intellectual if not architectural—was Les Invalides in Paris. The Royal Hospital was completed in 1687, making it older by a few years than Chelsea Hospital in London. The architect of this splendid building was William Robinson, the surveyor-general of Ireland. (He was also the designer of Marsh's Library, beside St Patrick's Cathedral.) It occupies an elevated site well to the west of the seventeenth-century city, standing to the south of the river, looking north across to the Phoenix Park on the other bank.

The arcaded inner quadrangle has a distinctly Italian feel to it and its cool classicism is in sharp contrast to the Baroque exuberance of the chapel. It fulfilled its original function until 1927. Following two generations of neglect, it was restored and now houses the Irish Museum of Modern Art.

Institutional developments indicated the city's growth, a trend which was most evident in the increased population, which stood at 50,000 by 1700. The first College of Physicians dates from 1667. Custom Houses were built and renewed, first in 1637 and again 30 years later, marking the growth in the city's seaborne commerce. After the building of Capel Street Bridge, it became necessary to move the Custom House to the east of it and the building of 1707 occupied the site of the modern Clarence Hotel before itself being replaced by the present building, Gandon's masterpiece of 1791. The

1707 Custom House was also the first to be built outside the city walls, a significant moment in itself, indicating a growing confidence in the political and military stability of the city. Once again, the growth of Dublin's trade was marked by physical expansion eastward towards the bay.

The upheaval in England known as the Glorious Revolution—it was actually a *coup d'état*—saw Charles II's Catholic brother, James II, dethroned in favour of his Protestant nephew, William of Orange, in order to protect the Protestant nature of the state and obviate a Catholic dynasty. While this period saw much upheaval in Ireland—James II's three years on the throne had revived hopes of undoing the Cromwellian settlement —little of it affected Dublin. The completeness of the Williamite victory at the Boyne and Aughrim—the latter the effective end of Old English Catholic resistance to the new order—was a reassurance to the Protestant city.

The opening of the new north–south axis across Capel Street Bridge, noted earlier, led to the development of Capel Street in the last quarter of the seventeenth century. It was named for Arthur Capel, Earl of Essex, lord lieutenant from 1672 to 1677. Developed by Sir Humphrey Jervis (a parallel street recalls his name), later lord mayor of the city, it quickly established itself as a centre of fashion and the *beau monde*. Moreover, it led to the area of Henrietta Street, where the first great Georgian developments were to take place in the 1720s and confirmed the north side—for the moment at least—as the fashionable end of town.

As the seventeenth century turned into the eighteenth and Dublin stood at the beginning of its heroic period, it could reflect with some satisfaction on the preceding half-century. Cromwell had, albeit with exemplary brutality, ended the state of flux that had existed in Ireland since the Silken Thomas rebellion over a century before. The Restoration and the brief reign of James II had not disturbed the basic settlement reached in the 1650s. The trade and commerce of the city had revived, especially following the arrival of Ormond and the stabilising of normal administration and government. Public spaces were opened up, new bridges spanned the river, Protestant immigrants from France brought new skills and energies to the city's economy, growing wealth was visible in the early development of new city quarters and the Royal Hospital was a symbol in stone of the arrival of the continental Renaissance in Ireland.

It all represented a startling and welcome contrast to the uncertainty and stasis that had plagued the city for 300 years since the Black Death. In reality, that is how long the recovery took, as Dublin moved from trading port to royal stronghold to national capital. For that was what it became in the eighteenth century, as the descendants of the Cromwellian settlers grew ever more assured in their victory. Their assurance expressed itself increasingly in a noisy campaign for colonial home rule, asserting the constitutional independence of the kingdom of Ireland from its bigger sister (an assertion that the bigger sister scorned for as long as she could).

It was this class, bound by ties of blood, ethnicity and

religion, that dominated the fortunes of eighteenth-century Ireland, in the process raising the capital to European status in population, wealth and beauty alike. They were an all-powerful minority, English by origin, Anglican in religion in a country in which 90 per cent of the population remained Roman Catholic, and alone constituting the political nation. It was not until the 1790s, when their hegemony was about to be fatally challenged, that they acquired the sobriquet by which they are remembered in history. But it is hardly ana-chronistic to apply it retrospectively. The eighteenth century was the age of the Ascendancy.

06 | THE ASCENDANCY CAPITAL

I n 1707 parliament passed 'An Act for Cleansing the Port, Harbour, and River of Dublin and for Erecting a Ballast Office in the said city'. The key functions of the Ballast Office were the imposition of port charges and the maintenance of the navigation channel. It continued the progressive embanking of the river. The construction of the quays on the north bank of the river, collectively known as the North Wall, was completed in less than 20 years. Charles Brooking's map of 1728 clearly shows a continuous embanking wall running from around the site of the modern Custom House to a point opposite Ringsend, roughly where the O_2 Arena stands today. The East Wall was an extension of the North Wall following the line of the present East Wall Road around to Ballybough.

The North and East Walls required constant renewal and maintenance and were greatly improved in the nineteenth century, when civil engineering skills were more advanced. But the construction of the originals in such an impressively short time was evidence of the energy which the early Ballast Office brought to the discharge of its duties.

It did not stop there. As early as 1715, it turned its attention to the south shore and began the construction of what was eventually to become the Great South Wall. Work started on this heroic project as early as 1716. The Ballast Office showed great consistency of purpose over a long period of time in the face of formidable practical difficulties. By 1731, the basic structure was complete from the Pigeon House to the Poolbeg. A lightship marked the eastern end, but it was rickety and unsatis-factory in practice. The disturbance of wind and tides was often too much for the timber wall. Individual piles were displaced and needed constant maintenance. Moreover, the uncertain mooring of the lightship presented a near-insoluble problem.

This is turn raised the question of a permanent lighthouse as the only effective substitute. The Ballast Office first proposed it in 1736. The idea got nowhere; it was raised again in 1744 with similar results. It was not until 1759 that the piles themselves were acknowledged to be an inadequate solution and the decision was taken to build a stone wall. The design incorporated a pro-vision for a lighthouse foundation at the eastern end.

The abutment for the lighthouse foundation was built first and then construction of the wall proceeded from east to west, or back towards the city. It took over 30 years to carry the wall all the way up to the site of the present O'Connell Bridge, but the lighthouse was finished and functioning as early as 1767. The Great South Wall is one of the finest engineering and construction achievements in the city's history. It is in its way as splendid a memorial of the city's golden age as any Georgian square or municipal building.

The final enclosing wall in Dublin Bay, the Bull Wall from Clontarf to the green North Bull Lighthouse, was first proposed in 1786 but not begun until 1819. It took five years to construct. It had two effects, one intended and the other not. The intended effect was to create a pincer in the bay, to narrow the navigation channel by bringing the Bull Wall to a point opposite to the Poolbeg lighthouse and thus creating what it was hoped would be a self-scouring and self-dredging system as the tides ebbed and flowed. This ambition was largely fulfilled, especially on the ebb tides.

The unexpected consequence was that the North Bull sandbank in the lee of the new wall began to stand proud at high tide and form itself into the Bull Island. The process was first noticed in the 1820s, almost as soon as the wall was completed. Instead of sand being washed into the harbour itself, it was now retained by the wall, thus adding to the existing bank. It grew in the course of the nineteenth century, by the end of which it was almost 5 km in extent and 6 metres above high water at its highest point. It now accommodates two 18-hole golf courses and is one of the country's most important bird and wildlife sanctuaries. On the seaward side, its beach—named Dollymount for the nearest suburb—is a major public amenity, by far the most splendid beach within the city boundary.

————

With the revival of the city's economic fortunes from the late seventeenth century on, wealthy and enterprising merchants and businessmen began to acquire parcels of land outside the walls with a view to property development. None were more influential than the three generations of the Gardiner family. The patriarch, Luke Gardiner (d. 1755), was a banker who married into the aristocratic Mountjoy family. He oversaw the early development of the Gardiner estate in the north-east of the city during the first half of the century. His grandson, also Luke, Lord Mountjoy (1745–98), was the principal figure in the second half.

Luke Gardiner the Elder first developed the area at the northern end of Capel Street. Bolton Street dates from 1720, but the real triumph was Henrietta Street, dating from a few years later. Here Gardiner built enormous town houses, vastly more spacious than anything else put up in the Georgian era. One of the first residents was Hugh Boulter, archbishop of Armagh, a key political and social figure of the day. Fashion—not least clerical fashion—followed him. Before long, Henrietta Street was known colloquially as Primate's Hill. It helped to establish the north-east suburbs of the city as the centre of early fashionable life. The drift of the *beau monde* to the south side did not start in earnest until the second half of the century.

This Luke Gardiner was also responsible for the development of Gardiner's Mall, later to mutate into Sackville Street and later again to O'Connell Street. When Gardiner acquired it, it was known as Drogheda Street (or Lane). This was named for Henry Moore, Earl of Drogheda, who is also commemorated in Henry Street, Moore Street, Earl Street and Of Lane, all of which have survived. Gardiner widened it by knocking down many of the existing properties and creating a central mall that ran from what is now Parnell Street to the modern Spire. This central area was named Gardiner's Mall, the two parallel sides Sackville Street—named for Lionel Sackville, Duke of Dorset, lord lieutenant in the 1730s. The unwidened lower end retained the name Drogheda Street until the extension of Sackville Street to the river in the 1780s. Meanwhile the lord lieutenant was further immortalised in Dorset Street, which was developed (but not by Gardiner) along the line of the old Drumcondra Lane, the traditional city exit to the north.

Shortly before his death, Luke Gardiner the Elder began the development of Rutland Square (now Parnell Square), which in time became a major centre of fashion, never more so than when Lord Charlemont built his town house in Portland stone—to distinguish it from the mere brick of the mansions adjacent—in the 1760s. It is now the Hugh Lane Gallery.

At the corner of Rutland Square nearest the top of Sackville Street, Bartholomew Mosse acquired four acres of land in 1748. Mosse was the proprietor of the Lying-In Hospital, the first dedicated maternity hospital in the world, which he had founded in George's Lane (now South Great George's Street) three years earlier. On this site he planned to build a larger maternity hospital and he engaged Richard Cassels, a German Huguenot who established himself as the leading Dublin architect of the 1730s and 1740s. The Rotunda—a Dublin landmark ever since—opened on 8 December 1757.

The first half of the eighteenth century saw an explosion of public building, some of the very highest quality. The new Parliament House opened to the design of Edward Lovett Pearce in the 1730s, although the additions by Gandon and others from the 1780s give the building its modern appearance. Pearce's original structure was one of classical purity and dramatic confidence.

Across the street, Trinity began to assume its modern form. The oldest surviving structure in the college, the Rubrics, dates from the first decade of the century. In the second, Thomas Burgh designed the Old Library. There are still prints that show it in the form in which Burgh left it, but its modern form derives from Deane and Woodward's addition of the sensational barrel-vaulted ceiling in the 1860s. Trinity was a work in progress for most of the century. The Printing House— a pretty building in the style of a Doric temple, the work of Cassels—dates from 1734. The Dining Hall followed in the next decade. The 1750s brought the great west front of the college giving onto College Green. Front Square itself was gradually completed in the 1780s. The Provost's House (1759) is the only private Georgian house in Dublin that still serves its original function.

Civic institutions of all kinds were founded in what was a display of growing urban self-possession. Jervis Street Hospital started life as the Charitable Infirmary (1718) in Cook Street before eventually settling in its eponymous location in 1796, where it stayed until it closed in 1987. St Patrick's Hospital was endowed by proceeds from Jonathan Swift's will—he died in 1745— and opened in 1757. It was the first psychiatric facility in Ireland and only the second in the British Isles.

The Dublin Society—later the Royal Dublin Society (RDS)—dates from 1731. The full title was the Dublin Society for the Improvement of Husbandry, Manufacturing and other Useful Arts. It was founded by fourteen gentlemen of learning, of whom Thomas Prior was the most notable. It was a typical product of the early Enlightenment: a voluntary association of private members, dedicated to the rational improvement of the applied arts. Its direct contribution to the life of the city is most easily set out in a list of the subsidiary entities established under its aegis: the Botanic Gardens (1795); Dublin's first school of art (1740s); its first museum (1790s), the remote ancestor of the National Museum of Ireland; the Natural History Museum; and the National Library of Ireland (1877), whose founding collection was based in large part upon the library of the RDS, which was transferred to the new institution.

Five years after the foundation of the RDS, the city had its first newspaper, the *Dublin Daily Advertiser*, but it was not until the first publication of the *Freeman's Journal* in 1763 that the city acquired a continuous journalistic voice.

———

We have mentioned Jonathan Swift only in passing, but no overview of Dublin in the first half of the eighteenth century is complete without him. He was born in Dublin in 1667. Both parents were English, although his maternal grandparents had themselves lived in Ireland in the 1630s. Swift's father was an official in the King's Inns in Dublin. The family was well connected: they were related to the Duke of Ormond on Swift's mother's side and were close to the Master of the Rolls in London, Sir John Temple, whose son, Sir William Temple, would become Jonathan Swift's influential patron as a young man.

The Swifts were therefore typical of many English families that established themselves in Dublin following the Restoration—the Ormond connection, in particular, would have done them no harm—and prospered with the developing city. The elder Swift died a few months before his son was born. The family memory of persecution by the Puritans in Cromwell's time—what Swift himself described as 'the barbarity of Cromwell's hellish crew'—inclined them towards an orthodox mainstream Anglicanism. This was the tradition into which Jonathan Swift was born. He was educated at Kilkenny grammar school and ordained in the church in 1695.

He was an ambitious clergyman and his ambition was firmly fixed on the larger island. In the first decade of the eighteenth century, he was in London and was an influential figure in literary and political circles. He wrote for *The Tatler,* and was a friend of Pope and other leading wits and artists. Politically, he hitched his star to the Tories but the death of Queen Anne ushered in the long Whig hegemony and Tory sympathisers were out of favour. Swift had backed the wrong horse. Instead of an appointment to the bench of bishops in the Church of England, which he had hoped for, he was returned to Dublin as a mere dean, albeit Dean of St Patrick's Cathedral.

For Swift, this was no homecoming: it was exile. He had harboured thoughts of a glittering career in the metropolis but had to settle for provincial Dublin instead. The ripening of Swift's satirical genius had this background for context. The Swifts were nominally Irish, but really English in Ireland and thinly rooted there. And the patriotism that Jonathan Swift was to espouse and personify from the 1720s on was that of the frustrated provincial, the creole abandoned by the metropole, condescended to and dismissed as of lesser account. Much of what was denominated patriotism in the eighteenth century—culminating in Grattan's Parliament in the last two decades—was of this kind. When an existential threat to this settler community arose in the wake of the French Revolution, the façade collapsed with suggestive ease.

None the less, the fact that a truculent colonial patriotism did develop was a testimony to the increasingly confident position of the New English elite in the early eighteenth century. They represented less than 10 per cent of the Irish population; they were observant Church of Ireland in their confessional allegiance, surrounded by a sea of Roman Catholics and—in their Ulster redoubt—Presbyterians. In a manner typical of pre-industrial states, this elite alone constituted the political nation. Their victory in the Williamite wars at the end of the preceding century had delivered them the security that made their position seem impregnable. This sense of security was the essential condition for their patriotism, because a nervous or insecure community could not have afforded the luxury of anti-English sentiment. This sentiment found some of its most virulent expression in the controversy known as Wood's Halfpence.

William Wood was an ironmaster in Wolverhampton, near Birmingham. In 1722, he was awarded a patent to mint £100,000's worth of copper coin for Ireland. This patent aroused immediate and spirited opposition in Ireland, where there was no national mint. It was alleged that he received the patent by paying £10,000 to the Duchess of Kendal, one of the king's mistresses. The total amount of currency in circulation in Ireland was about £400,000, so there was an understandable fear that Wood's coins would flood the country and cause a severe inflation.

That was the primary objection to the coinage, but there was also a sense of resentment that the Irish parliament had been bypassed yet again. The entire Irish establishment united against the coinage and refused to circulate it. In 1725, the London government admitted defeat and withdrew the patent. In the meantime, Swift had established himself as a master satirist by writing the six pamphlets collectively known as *The Drapier's Letters*. Assuming the disguise of M.B. Drapier, a respectable shopkeeper, Swift attacked the patent, but reserved his most acid and brilliant ridicule for the demeaning and subordinate position in which the colonial parliament was held.

The letters were addressed quite self-consciously to a Protestant audience, in an age when Dublin was still a Protestant city. Swift should not be confused with the later tradition of patriotism in the Irish nationalist context of the nineteenth and twentieth centuries. There was a common anti-English sentiment, but there the similarities end. Swift would almost certainly have been a unionist in the nineteenth century: the vast majority of the descendants of those he addressed in his satires were. Where he does represent the beginning of a tradition, however, is in the literary sense. He is the first in a line of Irish—usually Dublin—writers who have, whether in Ireland or overseas, been the island's glory. He stands at the head of a great tradition, one of the writers of true world importance that the city has produced.

By the mid century, Dublin had a population of about 150,000. It had grown to be the largest city in Britain or Ireland apart from London. The early pre-eminence of the north side was gradually reversed. The key moment in this was the decision by the Duke of Leinster—Ireland's only duke—to locate his town house in the south-east quarter. The building of Leinster House had exactly the effect that the duke had predicted: fashion followed him south. Within a few years, Merrion Square was being laid out and the city was assuming its modern shape. While the north side did not lose its social cachet until the nineteenth century, the south side was now firmly established as the more fashionable quarter. It has never lost that status.

The contrasts that are characteristic of any city at any time were never far away. In 1740 and 1741, there were bread riots in Dublin, as the whole island was gripped by a famine which proportionally was probably more severe than the Great Famine of the 1840s. It is estimated that up to 400,000 people died of starvation and consequent illnesses in these years, out of a total population of about 2.5 million. But just a year later, in 1742, Dublin played host to one of the great first performances in the history of European music. On 13 April, under the direction of the composer, Handel's *Messiah* was first performed in the New Musick Hall in Fishamble Street.

Such were the opposites typical of eighteenth-century European societies: on the one hand, the desperate subsistence crisis; on the other, ducal magnificence and artistic triumph. For by now, Dublin was truly reckoned to be a major European city. One visitor in the 1730s calculated that only London, Paris, Rome and Amsterdam had greater populations. He might have added Naples and a few others, but the general point was valid. By the mid-century, Dublin was established in the front rank of European cities.

07 | THE MID-EIGHTEENTH CENTURY

The establishment of the Wide Streets Commissioners in 1757 was the most enlightened piece of planning legislation the city's history. The body it set up was charged with widening existing narrow streets and proposing standards for new ones. It was empowered to buy land and property where necessary. The Commissioners were all men of substance and influence. What they created was a city re-imagined as an aristocratic display space, no longer simply the random, twisting pattern of streets dictated by ancient pathways and commercial necessity.

The modern city is unimaginable without their work. All the classic Georgian squares and streets on both side of the river felt their influence. Merrion Square is the prime example: the view down the south side of the square and along Upper Mount Street to the perspective point of the Pepper Canister Church is the best formal testimony to their purpose. They had real powers—they could override the Corporation in those areas within their remit—and they did not hesitate to use them.

They widened Lower Sackville Street down to the river and on the far side of Carlisle (now O'Connell) Bridge created the triangle of D'Olier Street, College Street and Westmoreland Street. They built Parliament Street to give better access to the Castle and widened Skinner's Row, one of the narrowest choke points in the old city, to create Christchurch Place. Dame Street owes its width to them. Oddly, they did not join the top of Dame Street to Christchurch Place, preferring instead to retain the narrow Castle Street link that survived from medieval times. Lord Edward Street, which filled this lacuna, was not punched through until the 1880s. On the approaches to the city, Baggot Street, Dorset Street and James's Street all owe their width to the Commissioners.

The remarkable formal unity of Georgian Dublin is a further product of their work. The great squares—Merrion and Fitzwilliam on the south side and Rutland (now Parnell) and Mountjoy on the north—plus their surrounding streets are clearly part of a common architectural vision. Even the north-side streets and squares, much reduced in beauty by a century of decay, neglect and vandalism, still bear testimony to that vision. The effect was to girdle the old city with a series of rectilinear processional and leisure spaces on its eastern and northern margins, with a visual consistency that is the city's thumbprint.

The new city was to be embraced by the arms of two

canals. On the south side, the Grand Canal was started in the 1750s. It linked Dublin to the River Shannon and also provided the city with an enhanced supply of potable water from two holding basins in the suburbs. The first commercial traffic started in 1779 and a passenger service began the following year. The company built a series of hotels along the route. By the end of the century, the canal had linked to the mouth of the Liffey at Ringsend and the Grand Canal Dock was built.

On the north side, the Royal Canal was not completed until 1817, the first barge having sailed in 1806. It was never as successful as the Grand and its later arrival left it even more vulnerable to the railway revolution in the mid-nineteenth century.

The classical eighteenth-century city was contained within the arms of the canals, with the Victorian suburban developments of the next century spreading beyond them. Shadowing the canals and running in rough parallel to them, the North and South Circular Roads date from the 1760s. One aspect of the Grand Canal was the branch extension that ran from Goldenbridge in the western approaches into the back of James's Street, to service the new brewery at St James's Gate. This was the source of Guinness, the most famous commercial product ever developed in the city, which dated from 1759.

By now, St Stephen's Green was being developed, with the north side (Beaux Walk) being especially fashionable. The west side was less so, due to the presence of a gallows near the corner of Cuffe Street, a reminder of how physically close were the *beau monde* and the *demi-monde* in an eighteenth-century city. A further physical survivor from the era prior to the development of the Green stands at the north-east corner, at the start of Merrion Row. The Huguenot Cemetery dates from 1693, when it would have been in an obscure, out-of-the-way location. However, it has maintained a continuous presence there ever since, although the last interment was in 1901. The lintel stone over the gate contains the most visible mis-spelling in the city, announcing the place as the Hughenot [sic] cemetery.

———

The story of eighteenth-century Dublin is usually told in terms similar to this narrative so far. It is the era of classical and aristocratic swagger, of heroic building projects, of the triumph of rational, Enlightenment town planning. And yes, it was all those things. But there was a dark face as well. Don't forget that gallows near Cuffe Street.

There was no city police force. Instead, there were a series of parish watches established under an Act of Parliament of 1723. Dublin was a violent city. Robbery, especially after dark, was a constant threat and pickpockets were ubiquitous. Beggars and vagrants were everywhere: the contrast between ascendancy style and the destitute poor was stark, as in much of the modern Third World. The English wit Samuel Foote, on a visit to the city, said that he had never known what English beggars did with their cast-off rags until he saw Irish beggars.

Sectarian rioting was a commonplace. The Liberty Boys—mainly Protestant weavers from the Liberties near St Patrick's Cathedral—fought regularly with the Ormond Boys—mostly Catholic butchers from the market on the north shore of the river. The whole summer of 1748 was given over to a series of affrays, many of them extremely violent and entailing horrendous injuries and fatalities. Nor was that the only such year: riots between the factions continued for the rest of the century.

Public holidays and fairs were also likely to be occasions of drunken rioting. The notorious Donnybrook Fair—originally sanctioned by royal charter as far back as 1204—had long since become one such. Essentially a horse fair, by the eighteenth century it had attracted various other forms of commerce, not the least of which was prostitution. In this connection, the city was very adequately stocked and had been for a long time. Attitudes to prostitution depended largely on the disposition of individual magistrates. The severity of the more moral (or moralising) was counterpointed by instances in which judicial leniency could best and most plausibly be explained by the Bench having prior acquaintance of the ladies arraigned before them. There were many instances of men being murdered in brothels, either by rivals or in some instances by the women themselves. Such incidents could lead to wholesale rioting, as in the case of Smock Alley in 1768. This street was home to the city's most famous theatre. It also contained, not entirely coincidentally in an age when actresses and prostitutes were thought to be one and the same, the greatest concentration of bawdy-houses. The 1768 riots went on for the best part of a week, resulted in the wholesale wrecking of suspected premises, and were only finally quelled by cavalry.

Brothels were ubiquitous in Dublin but the area around Christchurch was the focus of the trade. In Copper Alley, next to Smock Alley, a notorious brothel keeper, Darkey Kelly, was convicted in 1764 of murdering one of his clients and was burnt alive in the still half-developed Stephen's Green, within shouting distance of the fashionable Beaux Walk.

Mention of Beaux Walk is a reminder that crime and dissipation were not just the province of the poor. Dublin still had some of the air of a new-money frontier town, whose aristocracy was of recent establishment and accordingly coarse in its tastes. Dublin's 'Bucks'— young men of fashion and wealth much given to drunken dissipation, gambling and riot—were, in their own way, leaders of contemporary urban style. The most famous was Thomas 'Buck' Whaley, son of the MP Richard Chapell Whaley. The elder Whaley was a notorious religious bigot, who had to endure (or enjoy) the punning sobriquet 'Burn Chapel' in the light of his hatred and harassment of Roman Catholics. Like many a bad man, he did well out of public life and left his son a fortune when he died in 1769.

The boy—he was only three when his father died—wasted little time in blowing his inheritance. He followed his father into parliament at the age of 18 but spent most of his time at the gaming tables in the nearby Daly's Club, the resort of choice for the *jeunesse dorée* of the day. He continued to run through his money when he went to Paris and was forced back to Ireland. He won a bet by leaping out of the first-floor window of his palatial house at no. 86 St Stephen's Green straight into a waiting coach below. His most famous wager was reputedly for the colossal sum of £20,000, to win which he had to travel to Jerusalem and back in less than two years. He did it in nine months, an astonishing achievement in eighteenth-century travelling conditions. Of course, it made him famous. According to the charming but unreliable diarist Jonah Barrington, he took bribes from both sides to vote for and against the Act of Union. Barrington did the same thing himself.

It is one of the city's minor historical ironies that the Buck's great house, bequeathed him by his Papist-baiting father, passed into the hands of the church of Rome in the 1850s and became the first home of the new Catholic University, the antecedent to University College Dublin. It was renamed Newman House in honour of the cardinal who was the presiding founder of the university.

There were many other celebrated Bucks, not to mention the notoriously rowdy and lawless Trinity students, who were effectively above the law, being granted a sort of tribal indulgence denied to their less

fortunate fellow-townsmen. In a sense, the ferocity of
the punishments meted out to the criminal classes—the
hangings, burnings, pillories, transportation, whippings
(whether at whipping posts or through the streets)—
were a distorting mirror for the excesses of the cosseted
elite. The behaviour of the latter was as brutal in its way
as the punishments of the courts. The temper of
Georgian Dublin, once you got a little under the
glittering surface, was nervous, raw and provincial.

———

If it were possible to travel back in time, the first thing
that would strike any modern person transported to an
eighteenth-century city would be the smell. There were
no sewers. Waste, whether human faeces or dirty water
generally, was collected in cesspits. These were cylin-
drical tanks dug into the earth and filled with refuse.
They were covered and required to be emptied on a
regular basis as they filled up. Each house had its own
cesspit and the aggregate effect, especially in warm
summer weather, was overpowering. Moreover, the pits
attracted flies and vermin. It is hardly to be wondered
that the rich fled to the country for the summer to
escape the stink.

Dublin was no different to anywhere else in this
regard. As late as 1853, George Halpin, the inspector of
works for the Ballast Board, declared that 'the Liffey is
still the great main drain into which the sewerage of

Dublin opens'. Scavengers and night soil men (shit-collectors who either dumped their cargo in the river or sold it on for fertiliser) were employed by the city authorities to keep the cesspits serviced and the streets otherwise as clean as possible.

There were other hazards. The city was dark at night, facilitating the various criminal elements who preyed on the unwary. A system of public lanterns in the city centre, maintained at the residents' expense, was gradually developed but it was a very partial answer to a larger problem, the real solution of which had to await the development of the electric light in the next century.

Fire was a constant concern, especially in the older parts of the city which still contained a great number of wooden buildings. A primitive fire-fighting service dates from 1706 and the earliest fire insurance scheme from 1740, at which time fire insurance was well established in Britain.

In all, the Georgian city was a place of violent contrasts. It was still, in every sense, a work in progress. When the Dublin parliament gained 'legislative independence' from Westminster in 1782, there was as yet no Custom House or Four Courts or Fitzwilliam or Mountjoy Squares. There was a primitive piped water system, no main drainage or proper street lighting and a subculture of violence common to Bucks and criminals alike, unchallenged by a municipal police force. Many of these absences were simply a product of their time and were common to all of Europe. Some were, in whole or in part, due to Dublin's relative newness as a significant city.

But a significant city it was. And the last quarter of the eighteenth century was to be regarded ever after as its golden age.

08 THE SUNSET OF THE CLASSICAL CITY

The Old Pretender, son of King James II, died in 1766, at which point Pope Clement XIII regarded the Stuarts as a busted flush and formally acknowledged the Hanoverian George III as the legitimate king. The final removal of the chance of a Stuart restoration had the effect of making the ascendancy even more secure in its historic triumph.

But security breeds another kind of confidence, the kind that allows for internal dissentions that had been suppressed in times of greater danger. The emergence of the so-called patriot interest in the Irish parliament in the last third of the century was no coincidence. Patriotism has often been called 'colonial nationalism'. It represented a sensibility among some members of the ascendancy that Irish colonial interests had been subordinated to English interests, and that the larger kingdom had been oppressive and selfish in its dealings with the smaller.

Restrictions on the Irish cattle and woollen trades were resented, as was the regular practice of awarding plum positions in church and state to English candidates rather than Irish. Parliament itself was subordinate to Westminster. The argument was made that Ireland was a separate kingdom which should be ruled by her own people (meaning the Anglican elite who alone con- stituted the political nation in a pre-democratic age). These sentiments had been present throughout the century—the Wood's Halfpence affair being the best example from an earlier generation—but the growing self-assurance of the ascendancy as a whole gave them renewed oxygen.

Benjamin Franklin visited Ireland in 1771 and found among the Irish patriots men of a similar temper to those Americans who chafed under British colonial exactions. When the American Revolution broke out four years later, it found ready support among ascend- ancy radicals. They forced the London government to abolish Irish export restrictions, so long a cause of tension between the two sides. The London government pulled regular troops out of Ireland to fight in America, leaving the country under-protected. Into this gap flowed a newly-formed Irish Volunteer force, which began to mobilise in 1778. It was an entirely Protestant body under landlord leadership and by 1779 it numbered about 40,000 members. This number increased by a half to 60,000 by 1782. It proved to be a powerful persuader for further concessions from London. In effect, the Irish patriots now had their own volunteer army.

They duly achieved their goal in 1782 when the Irish parliament achieved its 'independence' of Westminster. The statutes that had made Dublin subordinate legislatively were repealed and The Old House on College Green—as it was to be known in romance thereafter—entered into its brief pomp. It may have been free of Westminster, but it was not free of the Dublin Castle administration, which for the most part had no truck with patriot sentiment and which still controlled the levers of administrative power. There was a never-resolved tension between the two ends of Dame Street.

There were liberal elements in the Volunteer/patriot movement who wished to lessen Catholic legal disabilities. Gardiner's relief acts of 1778 and 1782 represented the first formal easing of the Penal Laws. But there were also significant figures among the patriots who feared such liberal reforms. This difference of opinion was to prove significant in 1800, at the time of the Act of Union. And outside the ranks of the patriots, ascendancy figures more closely associated with the Castle administration—powerful figures like the attorney-general John Fitzgibbon, later lord chancellor under the title Lord Clare—were adamantine in their opposition to Catholic relief and nervous about any further weakening of the connection with England.

These factions were not just political in the larger sense. They also echoed some of the controversies concerning the ongoing development of the city of Dublin. Plans to continue the eastward development of the city were the cause of bitter public controversy. The building of the Custom House—now regarded as the finest single classical structure in the city—was especially so. The architect James Gandon was a protégé of John Beresford, the First Commissioner of Revenue and an important and influential figure in the Castle administration. In tandem with Luke Gardiner, Beresford developed the area of Lower Gardiner Street, Lower Abbey Street and Beresford Place as well as the Custom House itself.

Beresford's position in the Castle was enough to arouse patriot opposition to his plans, opposition which was echoed by merchant interests which did not want any further eastward drift of the city's commerce. The most prominent of the patriots, Henry Grattan, was a vociferous opponent of the new Custom House. So was James Napper Tandy, one of the founders of the United Irishmen. The city mob was mobilised in opposition, to the point where Gandon felt obliged to wear a sword when visiting the site. None the less, the work proceeded and by 1791, after 10 years of heroic labour on a site which was all reclaimed slob-land, the great Custom House was completed. It is impossible to think of modern Dublin without it.

There is little doubt that Gardiner and Beresford, each of them members of the Wide Streets Commission, abused their positions in order to profit from the development of lands which they owned. By any modern standards, their conduct was self-serving if not downright corrupt and one can more readily understand the otherwise incomprehensible opposition to the Custom House when one bears this in mind. Moreover, it was seen as Beresford's personal project, and Beresford was both high-handed and deeply unpopular. He has also been vindicated by the outcome, which may be insufficient justification for the squeamish, but is its own reward.

Gandon was *the* architect of Dublin golden age. The only rival that the Custom House faces for the prize of greatest building in the city is his Four Courts, built farther upstream on the north bank of the river, near the ancient *Átha Cliath* from which the city takes its Irish-language name. This monumental structure dominates the upper reaches of the river. The foundation stone was laid in 1786 and the building was finished in 1801, although it was sufficiently advanced by 1796 for the courts to use it.

He was also responsible for the brilliantly successful eastern addition to Lovett Pearce's Parliament House. This created a new entrance to the House of Lords with its portico and Corinthian columns projected over the street pavement. The pavement in question in 1789, when this work was completed, was that of Fleet Lane, a narrow thoroughfare that crossed Fleet Street and terminated at the river on Aston Quay.

Fleet Lane soon became Westmoreland Street. As part

of the last major undertaking sponsored by the Wide Streets Commissioners, the river was bridged at the end of Sackville Street when Carlisle Bridge was opened in 1795. Two new streets were built to complete the connection of the Gardiner and Beresford estates on the north side, centred on Sackville Street, to the Parliament House and Trinity. Westmoreland Street and D'Olier Street date from the early years of the nineteenth century, but their genesis lay in the closing years of the old century. They gave the city a new central north–south axis which it has never lost.

Gandon was also partly responsible for the design of the King's Inns at the head of Henrietta Street, the other architect being his pupil Henry Aaron Baker. It is a fine building but occupies a part of the city that was to suffer badly during the nineteenth-century decline and has hardly felt any effect from the so-called Celtic Tiger boom of the 1990s and 2000s. It stands as a distinguished orphan in an otherwise neglected and shabby urban environment.

This western end of the Gardiner estate was one of the more conspicuous areas where the energy gave out. Plans to build a royal circus at the far end of Eccles Street, where the Mater Hospital and Berkeley Street church now stand, were never realised. This early decline on the western fringe of the city was, in a sense, the mirror image of continuing developments to the east. The Merrion/Pembroke estate, in particular, continued to demonstrate its vitality in the development of Fitzwilliam Square, the last of the classical Dublin squares to be constructed. Begun in the 1790s, it was not completed until the 1820s. It is smaller and more intimate than its near neighbour, Merrion Square, or than Mountjoy Square on the north side. Its charm is largely a function of this smaller size.

On its eastern flank, the square is an extension of Upper Fitzwilliam Street, which, together with Lower Fitzwilliam Street and Fitzwilliam Place, runs from the south-east corner of Merrion Square across the junction with Baggot Street and all the way up to Leeson Street. The entire vista thus created was over a kilometre long and—subject to a few footling variations of theme here and there—uniformly classical. It was by far the longest continuous Georgian streetscape in Dublin and one of the longest anywhere. It survived as such until the barbarism of the 1960s—that deadly decade for architecture—disturbed its uniformity.

Among the other buildings of classical Dublin that were neither developed by the great estates nor designed by James Gandon, the Royal Exchange deserves particular mention. With the development of Dame Street and the building of Parliament Street, the site at the junction of these streets acquired a strategic and visual importance it had previously lacked. This was the site chosen for a new Royal Exchange to replace the previous building in Winetavern Street. It was a meeting place for the traders and merchants of the city to transact business, operating on the same essential principle as a modern stock exchange.

The competition to design the new Royal Exchange

was won by Thomas Cooley, a Londoner and one of the many architects busily engaged in the wholesale redevelopment of the nearby Castle and the creation of the Upper Castle Yard. Work began in 1769 and it took 10 years to build. The result is magnificent, one of the very finest buildings in Dublin, doing justice to its sensitive position enclosing the view along Capel Street, across the river and up Parliament Street. It ceased to discharge its original function in 1852 and has since served as the City Hall.

————

Classical Dublin was a city of contrasts, as is every city in every era. The superb streetscapes and noble public buildings were cheek-by-jowl with foetid slums and rank poverty. Ireland was still in many respects a marchland, a frontier land. Its aristocracy, according to Jonah Barrington's famous tripartite taxonomy, comprised Gentlemen to the Backbone, Gentlemen Every Inch of Them and Half-Mounted Gentlemen. Quite what the distinction was between the first two categories is obscure but there is no doubting the third. The hard-drinking, hard-gambling, roistering, duelling squireens were the Half-Mounted element. Their urban equivalents were the Bucks and pinkindindies, and the wild young men in Daly's Club on College Green whose idea of amusement was to take pot-shots at the statues in the grounds of St Andrew's Church nearby. The roaring boys were as emblematic of the time as the cultivated gentlemen.

At the centre of the city's life stood parliament, the Old House on College Green. An Irish parliament had existed since the thirteenth century, for most of its existence limited and circumscribed in its powers. But since the winning of legislative independence in 1782, it was a real force in the land. The rising of the United Irishmen in 1798 shattered the complacent certainties of its world and of the ascendancy world generally. Panicked by an insurrection that seemed to combine a nightmare junction of Catholic peasant revival and French revolutionary principles, the ascendancy was persuaded and bribed to abolish its own parliament and effect a union with Great Britain. The two kingdoms would now be one, the United Kingdom. So it became on 1 January 1801. For Dublin, it was the end of the golden age.

09 | THE START OF THE LONG DECLINE

It is one of the great truisms of Dublin history that the city went into a steep decline after the Union. There is no arguing the point, although it will bear some qualification. The basic case is unanswerable. Once Dublin ceased to be a centre of independent—or at least autonomous—political power, ambition and style gravitated towards London. There was no longer any requirement to come to Dublin to attend parliament, so MPs, their servants, retainers and entourages found it easier to resettle in London, or to go there directly from their country estates, bypassing the capital.

This happened progressively over time. The effect was the gradual abandonment of many fine houses and their conversion to other purposes, not least—especially in the second half of the nineteenth century—to degraded tenement slums. This process was most marked in that north-western quadrant of the city that was the first to be abandoned by fashion. The canal basin at Broadstone—and later the railway station adjacent—brought commercial traffic into the heart of this area, further lowering its prestige. This process accounts for the distressed condition of Dominick Street by the late nineteenth century, when it was a conspicuous example of slum misery. Before the Union, it had been one of the noblest streets in the city.

The decisive movement of fashion was from northwest to south-east. The Pembroke/Fitzwilliam estate, centred on Merrion and Fitzwilliam Squares, retained their insulation from the unpleasant world of commerce. Moreover, the first railway in Ireland opened in 1834 on the northern margins of this estate at Westland Row and provided a new commuter link to the shoreline of the southern bay, from which followed gradual suburban development and the possibility of flight from the less pleasant aspects of the city—not least its taxes—to charming seaside villas.

By skirting the edge of the Pembroke/Fitzwilliam estate, this railway—the Dublin & South-Eastern—gave access to and from fashionable Dublin without impinging on it physically. In this, it contrasts with the other three main Dublin rail termini, all of which had a disimproving effect on their immediate areas, or accelerated a decline already present. The Great Northern terminus at Amiens Street (now Connolly) was on the edge of the Gardiner estate, already declining in prestige as fashion fled south. The Great Southern & Western's magnificent station at Kingsbridge (now Heuston) was at the western end of the Liffey quays, in a traditionally poor area. Likewise, we have noted the effect of the Midland Great Western terminus at Broadstone. In general, railway stations did nothing for the social prestige of their surroundings, in Dublin or anywhere else.

The gradual flight of wealth from north to south, and also out of the city altogether, left a greater proportion of the poor and impoverished behind, and emphasised with stark clarity just how desperate life at the bottom was. The best and earliest testimony we have comes from the reports of a heroic clergyman, Rev. James Whitelaw. As early as 1805, he produced a report based on his many visitations to the homes of the poor. The scenes he described and the causes to which he ascribed the wretched poverty and ill-health of the Dublin poor were to find echoes throughout the nineteenth century and beyond.

He described conditions of incredible overcrowding, with sometimes even single rooms being subdivided to provide a minimal and miserable living space. He left graphic and disgusting accounts of the complete absence of any sanitary clearance system and the consequent concentration of dung heaps—for human and animal waste alike—and rubbish middens in enclosed back yards. One quotation from his 1805 report will suffice: 'Into the back-yard of each house, frequently not ten feet deep, is flung from the windows of each apartment the ordure and filth of its numerous inhabitants; from whence that it is so seldom removed that I have seen it on a level with the windows of the first floor; and the moisture that, after heavy rain, oozes from this heap, having frequently no sewer to carry it off, runs into the street by the entry leading to the staircase.'

Commercial activity such as brewing and soap manufacture also produced noxious or filthy by-products. There were lime-kilns in residential areas. There were open sewers everywhere in poor areas. People living in vastly overcrowded conditions and in close proximity to such ubiquitous filth were obviously prone to infectious diseases, the causes of which were still not properly understood or acknowledged. For example, there were devastating outbreaks of cholera in 1818 and 1832.

In addition, the city was still small, almost wholly contained between the two canals. In this limited space, the population had risen to more than 200,000 people. Even with growing social segregation, wealth and poverty were uncomfortably close. Wealth demanded servants, and servants could carry infectious diseases from the slums to the homes of the mighty. Professions such as medicine and the clergy were especially vulnerable. Moreover, social segregation was incomplete. Even the wealthiest parts of the city had slums adjacent. The area immediately north of Merrion Square was one such, which is why it was all right for the Dublin & South-Eastern Railway to punch through the slums to its terminus at Westland Row. The area remains a poor one to this day.

The year 1803 brought one of the city's tragic romances. Robert Emmet had been well born, the son of the state physician. He was educated at Trinity, from which he was expelled in 1798—that climactic year—in a purge of radical undergraduates. He had joined the United Irishmen and when their rebellion (in which he played no part) failed, he maintained contact with some of the survivors. Following in the footsteps of Wolfe Tone, he went to France to solicit military aid from Napoleon for a further attempt. None was forthcoming and by the autumn of 1802 he was back in Ireland.

He hatched an elaborate plan to stage a *coup d'état* in Dublin when England was once more at war with France, which it was from early 1803. The plan entailed a raid for arms on the Pigeon House garrison at Ringsend which, when successful, would be announced by the firing of a rocket into the sky. This would be the signal for other bodies of rebels to rise. Emmet greatly exaggerated the number of potential supporters at his disposal by including numbers of the city's poor in his calculations. This caused some of the other potential leaders, including Michael Dwyer of Wicklow, a veteran of '98, to suspect Emmet's fitness for the role he had assumed. Dwyer was a dedicated revolutionary, and he had a distrust of potentially undisciplined mobs which would have not been amiss in the mouth of a regular army officer.

None of Emmet's elaborate plans materialised. Worse, on 16 July an arms depot in Patrick Street exploded, threatening to unravel and reveal the entire conspiracy.

This led Emmet to bring forward the date of the rising to 23 July and to focus only on an attempt to capture Dublin Castle. It was a fiasco. Emmet marched a group of eighty or so men, many of them the worse for drink, through the Liberties to Thomas Street, there to muster for an assault on the Castle. Dressed in a dashing green military jacket and a plumed hat, he tried to enthuse the local populace, which declined to be enthused. Realising the hopelessness of his situation, he abandoned the attempt on the Castle and fled south, towards Wicklow. Unfortunately, his men now turned into a leaderless mob and for about two hours they held Thomas Street and James's Street in what was effectively a riotous assembly.

By the time order was restored by troops from the Castle, about fifty people were killed, including the notably liberal Lord Kilwarden, the chief justice, and his nephew. They were piked to death by the mob. By a bitter irony, Kilwarden's family name was Wolfe: they were a landed family from Co. Kildare. In 1763, the head of the family had been one Theobald Wolfe, in whose honour one of his tenants, Peter Tone, a coachman, had named his eldest son.

Emmet's myth proceeds from the nature of his capture and death. He was in love with Sarah Curran, the daughter of John Philpott Curran, the most famous Irish barrister of the day and a man who had been personally close to the United men in 1798. Whether Sarah Curran requited Emmet's obvious devotion to her is uncertain, but his eventual capture by the authorities was due to his refusing safe passage to France until he could see her. Songs and ballads were written in memory of this doomed love, the best known of them Thomas Moore's 'She Is Far From the Land'.

Emmet then ensured his immortality in the Irish tradition with his speech from the dock following his inevitable conviction for high treason. It is one of the most famous speeches in Irish history. Emmet was hanged and beheaded in Thomas Street on 20 September and his body buried at Bully's Acre in the grounds of the Royal Hospital, Kilmainham. He was just 25.

————

The early years of the nineteenth century did not see the city simply collapse into a slough of poverty, rebellion and neglect. The Royal College of Surgeons in Ireland opened its splendid new building on the west side of St Stephen's Green in 1806, thus giving the least fashionable side of the Green a building of distinction. In Sackville Street, the Dublin architect *du jour,* Francis Johnston, built a new General Post Office (1814–18), which dominates the street to this day. Ironically, both the GPO and the College of Surgeons were to play key roles in the events of 1916, in which the spirit of Robert Emmet was so often invoked. Johnston was also principally responsible for Nelson Pillar (1808), the city's icon for more than a century and a half. The Pillar was blown up in 1966 by persons also inclined to invoke Emmet's ghost.

Another city icon, the Ha'penny Bridge, dates from 1816. It is formally known as Wellington Bridge, in memory of the victor of Waterloo the previous year, himself one of the city's more reluctant sons. It is also sometimes referred to as the Metal Bridge, and with some justice, because it is one of the earliest examples in Ireland of a single-span metal bridge. However, its most famous moniker refers to the toll of one halfpenny that was levied to cross it (it was and is purely a pedestrian bridge) from its opening until 1919. In 1820, a more substantial memorial to the Iron Duke was completed in the form of the Wellington Monument in the Phoenix Park, the biggest obelisk in Europe. It was built in three years, but did not assume its final appearance until the bronze panels commemorating Wellington's victories were put in place in 1861. They were cast from cannon captured in the Peninsular War.

In 1820, the long reign of King George III ended. He was succeeded by the former Prince Regent, now George IV, a dissipated sot. The new king visited Dublin in 1821, the first English king ever to visit Ireland for a wholly peaceful purpose. He arrived drunk.

The original intention had been to land at the new mail packet harbour of Dunleary, which was to be renamed Kingstown in his honour. However, he was so far gone in drink that it was felt that the waiting crowd would be scandalised by the sight of their sovereign in a distressed condition. He was taken across the bay to the fishing port of Howth and put ashore there. The point at the end of the west pier where he first trod on Irish soil is commemorated by an impressed set of his foot-prints, still present there.

The king's visit was a great success, although the man was racked by diarrhoea. He went to the Curragh races, where a vast travelling commode was provided for his sole use and was pressed into frequent and regular service. His Majesty departed as he had meant to come, through Kingstown, as it was now to be called for a century. His was the first of a series of occasional royal visits in the course of the nineteenth and early twentieth centuries: Queen Victoria, Edward VII and George V all visited the city.

In general, the first half of the nineteenth century is not regarded as one of Dublin's great eras. The shadow of the classical age lay too heavily across it. None the less, there were developments that were decisive for the future and significant in themselves. The opening of the Pro-Cathedral in 1825 was a public statement that the penal era was long in the past. While the established church still held the ancient cathedrals of Christ Church and St Patrick's and the new Catholic cathedral was obliged to locate itself discreetly in a quiet quarter parallel to Sackville Street, its official consecration was a seminal moment. Four years later, Daniel O'Connell had secured the passage of the Catholic Emancipation Act at Westminster, removing nearly all residual legal disabilities against Catholics. There followed an explosion of Catholic church-building during the rest of the century, as well as the development and expansion of Catholic schools, teaching orders and hospitals.

Dublin had ceased to be a Protestant city. Its Catholic majority was about to make its political voice heard.

In 1830, there was founded one of the city's most enduring and best-loved amenities, the Zoo. Situated then as now in the Phoenix Park, it is the oldest zoological gardens in the British Isles after Regent's Park in London. A less loved institution was formed in 1836 with the introduction of a new police service along the lines pioneered by the London Metropolitan Police (1829). The Irish Constabulary was formed as an armed *gendarmerie* for the country outside Dublin. The capital got its own unarmed force, the Dublin Metropolitan Police (DMP), at the same time, thus putting urban policing on a recognisably modern footing.

We have already noted the foundation of the Irish railway system, radiating from a Dublin hub, in 1834, and facilitating the development of the southern seaside suburbs. The spread of the railway system drew middle-class people away from the decaying city centre in the course of the century, resulting in the creation of a series of nine independent townships where local taxation was lighter than in the city. This was a serious development, for the city could ill afford the erosion of its revenue base given the scale of the social and economic problems it faced. In effect, the flight to the townships was the new middle class giving up on the city itself. The independent townships survived until 1930, when they were reincorporated into the metropolitan area.

City government did take a major step forward in 1840 as a result of the Municipal Corporations (Ireland) Act of that year. The net effect was to make city government more representative and less oligarchic. In place of the old series of nominating bodies, all of them exclusively Protestant, the Corporation was now elected by all rate-paying property owners. The measure had been part of a deal made between the Whig government in London and Daniel O'Connell, the hero of the Catholic Emancipation struggle and the champion of Irish nationalism. As a result of this measure, O'Connell became lord mayor of the city in the following year, the first Catholic to hold the office since 1688.

10 | VICTORIAN AND EDWARDIAN DUBLIN

The reform of municipal government meant the consolidation of power in Dublin Corporation. Regulatory functions which had previously been chaotically dispersed among individual parishes and voluntary bodies were now subject to greater central control. The most impressive results were seen in areas like sanitation and public health, where the second half of the century brought major advances. The first medical health officer for the city was appointed in 1864 and a huge step forward took place with the opening of the Vartry waterworks in 1863. For the first time, the city was provided with a pure water supply at high pressure, which was the envy of other, richer cities in Britain and abroad.

The chief promoter of this initiative was the chairman of the waterworks committee, Sir John Gray, whose statue stands in O'Connell Street. The Vartry's retaining dam held 11 million cubic metres, which then flowed through a 4-km-long tunnel to a large open service reservoir at Stillorgan before delivering up to 85,000 cubic metres daily to the city.

Hand in hand with this major advance in the city's infrastructure went the development of domestic plumbing systems and the city's sewer system. A Royal Commission on the Sewerage and Drainage of Dublin reported in 1880. It built on a sewerage system that had been begun in 1870 and was to develop into the Main Drainage Scheme in 1892, not reaching its full extent until 1906.

These developments were all the more urgent because of the growing population of the city, which was especially marked in the years following the catastrophic Great Famine of 1845–52. The city swelled with wretchedly poor people fleeing from the stricken countryside. This in turn accelerated the flight of the middle classes to the nine new townships: Rathmines & Rathgar, Pembroke, Blackrock, Kingstown, Dalkey, Killiney, Kilmainham, Drumcondra and Clontarf: all safely outside the ring of the two canals and therefore beyond the reach of the Corporation, each with its own local authority and town hall and with lower rates than the city.

The division of the classes is the big theme of Victorian Dublin. The poor remained in a decaying, hideously overcrowded centre, many living in conditions of squalor without parallel in northern Europe. The moneyed middle classes—ever more the social leaders of the city now that the flight of the old aristocracy was almost complete—lived in the townships, but worked, shopped and enjoyed concerts and theatres in the city to which they otherwise made no material contribution. As the city housing situation, especially in the tenements, went from bad to worse, with no clear plan for wholesale slum clearance, the suburbs witnessed a dramatic expansion with the development of delightful red-brick areas like Ranelagh, Ballsbridge, Blackrock and Kingstown. Later the north side followed suit with Drumcondra and Clontarf.

Dublin has as much claim to be a Victorian as a Georgian city. An assertively red-brick Victorian style dominates domestic suburban architecture from the 1860s. By 1891, the city population was just over 245,000, but that of the suburbs outside the Corporation area was already past 100,000. Those who could get out of town got out.

Having got out, of course, they needed to get back in for work and pleasure. In this regard, the development of the tramway system was crucial. The first commercial tram ran in Dublin in 1872, on a route from the city to Rathmines. The tramway system spread rapidly, soon overwhelming the primitive omnibus network that had preceded it. In 1891, the three existing companies were consolidated as the Dublin United Tramway Company, which ran the city's first electric tram in 1896. The DUTC survived until 1945, bequeathing its much-loved 'flying snail' logo to its unloved successor CIÉ.

Complementing access to and from the suburbs was

the suburban railway system. Lines operated by the principal mainline companies were gradually studded with suburban halts to serve commuters' needs. The series of south-side stations along the Dublin & South-Eastern line to Wexford still form the backbone of the modern DART service.

The last third of the nineteenth century was the decisive period of suburban expansion, facilitated by the transport revolution. An early observer of the system noted the preponderance of bourgeois passengers on the trams. Maurice Brooks MP, the proprietor of one of the city's longest-established building supply businesses, commented in 1879 that 'the Dublin Tram Company has turned out very remunerative and in some respects a very useful institution, excellent returns to its proprietors, and proving of great convenience to passengers of the genteel and well-to-do class'. He added that the company had 'failed to confer equal advantages on the working or labouring class' by reason of its scheduling times and high fares.

The period from the 1850s to the mid-1870s was the high noon of Victorian prosperity in Britain. In Ireland outside east Ulster, it was the generation of recovery from the trauma of the Great Famine. Yet some of the optimism of the bigger island rubbed off on Dublin. In 1853, a major industrial exhibition was held in the city, on the lawns of the Royal Dublin Society, the sponsoring institution, at Leinster House facing onto Merrion Square. It was opened by Queen Victoria and Prince Albert and was an echo of London's Great Exhibition of

1851 in the Crystal Palace. A contemporary engraving of the opening ceremony shows a structure which looks a mimic of the Crystal Palace: the Dublin structure was in fact timber framed. The products of industry were a novelty in the 1850s—the Industrial Revolution was still in its early days and mostly confined to Britain—and the Dublin exhibition was partly intended for display and partly mounted in the hope of accelerating the post-Famine recovery. Given the absence of an industrial base outside Ulster, this well-meaning gesture proved futile.

The following year brought a significant if little-noticed development. The Catholic University was founded, with Cardinal Newman as its first rector. It is the lineal antecedent of UCD, now the largest institution of higher learning in Ireland. It started life in 86 St Stephen's Green. Right beside it, Newman commissioned a college chapel and got a gem. John Hungerford Pollen's University Church is a mock-Byzantine reproach to Protestant ecclesiastical austerity, its exuberant ornamentation and mosaics an assertion of architectural values that mirror the liturgical theatricality of Roman Catholicism.

The appointment of Paul Cullen as Catholic Archbishop of Dublin in 1852 brought the most substantial cleric in nineteenth-century Ireland to the capital. An uncompromising Counter-Reformation Catholic, he had spent over twenty years as an influential figure in the Vatican before returning to Ireland. He was fearless, intelligent and formidable. He did little to soften sectarian tensions but he oversaw a huge institutional expansion of the church in the archdiocese during his 26 years in office. He encouraged the great expansion of Catholic education, a feature of the city's life throughout the century. The Catholic presence in the professions was most marked in medicine, with UCD's medical school at Cecilia Street in Temple Bar establishing an early reputation. The opening of the Mater Hospital (1861) at the top of Eccles Street on the fringes of the old Gardiner estate was a major event in the city's history. Rome rewarded Cullen in 1866 by making him the first Irish cardinal. Although he had no liking for British rule in Ireland, Cullen had even less time for nationalist secret societies, which explained his inveterate hatred for the Fenians, whose abortive rebellion of 1867—it was scarcely less farcical than Emmet's effort—he denounced. One of the Fenians, John O'Leary, later told W.B. Yeats that in Ireland a man must either have the Church or the Fenians on his side, a lesson that Cullen understood instinctively and Parnell was to learn the hard way in 1891.

———

The same year that Newman founded his university brought an end of a very old tradition: Donnybrook Fair. The medieval village of Donnybrook, long distant from the city, was by the 1850s firmly in the path of the southward expansion of the Pembroke township. The new residents had not fled the city to endure the riot of Donnybrook Fair. They bought out the original charter that was the legal sanction for the event, which was thereby suppressed.

This replacement of ancient riot by modernising order was at least as emblematic of the age as the continued chaos in the city's housing situation. As symbols of that order, the opening of the National Gallery of Ireland in 1864 and of the National Library and National Museum in 1890 represent key moments in the process of furnishing Dublin with a civic infrastructure. The Gallery was the product of the philanthropy of William Dargan, the railway engineer, who had bankrolled the 1853 exhibition and was reputed to have lost £20,000 in the process. The exhibition had included paintings, and the idea that there should be a city gallery took hold. The initial costs were met by public subscription and Dargan's seminal role was recalled by placing his statue outside the new building.

The Library and Museum were both products of legislation passed by parliament in 1877. In both instances, their core deposits were based on the holdings of the RDS and were specially donated for the purpose. The twin institutions occupied the wings of Leinster House, then the headquarters of the RDS. Another example of public-spirited philanthropy was the opening of the nearby St Stephen's Green as a public park in 1880. It had been the private domain of the Lords Iveagh, heirs to the Guinness fortune, prior to that.

In 1882, the Phoenix Park Murders shocked the city and the country and made international headlines. A group calling themselves the Invincibles, a Fenian off-shoot, butchered the new chief secretary, Lord Frederick Cavendish, and the under-secretary, Thomas Burke, within sight of the Viceregal Lodge. Cavendish was a nephew of Gladstone and had just arrived in Dublin to take up his appointment. Burke—the real target of the assassins—was the head of the Dublin Castle admin-istration. The long-term repercussions of this horrible crime included an attempt by the *Times* to implicate Charles Stewart Parnell, the unquestioned leader of Irish nationalism, by printing forged letters suggesting he had foreknowledge of the plot. The charge did not stand up to scrutiny and Parnell's vindication left his stock at an all-time high: he persuaded Gladstone to introduce a Home Rule Bill for Ireland in 1886 which would have restored the domestic autonomy of an Irish parliament. Although the measure was lost in Westminster, it seemed only a matter of time before it would succeed. Parnell's fall from grace in 1890–91 was all the greater for the height to which he had previously ascended. Dublin remained a Parnell stronghold to the end, and his funeral in October 1891 was one of the biggest and most moving the city has ever seen.

The years after the fall of Parnell are conventionally thought of as those in which culture displaced politics in nationalist Ireland. Certainly, the country and the city displayed a revived cultural vitality. The founding of the Gaelic League in 1893 influenced the new generation of nationalists in a manner hitherto unthinkable, stressing the importance of native custom and language. Cross-pollinated with politics in the revolutionary era to come, it made for a heady brew.

The founding of the Irish Literary Theatre in 1899 was followed five years later by the Abbey, giving Ireland what is usually said to be its national theatre. But while its general purpose served nationalism, it did not scruple to subvert nationalist shibboleths. Unlike the Gaelic League, which, although founded by the Protestant Douglas Hyde, was overwhelmingly Catholic in membership, the Abbey was a curious hybrid of Anglo-Irish mavericks and the nationalist mainstream, with the former in control. Yeats and Lady Gregory were the moving spirits and J.M. Synge the playwright of genius who made the theatre's reputation. In the process, he so offended nationalist piety in *The Playboy of the Western World* that the play sparked a famous riot, not entirely to Yeats's chagrin—for the poet was a bonny fighter and welcomed a chance to rebuke the multitude *de haut en bas.*

———

The second half of the nineteenth century saw a restructuring and expansion of Dublin Port, that critical artery in the city's economic life. Its governance was vested in a new Port & Docks Board in 1868. The opening of Alexandra Basin in 1885 added to the port's capacity and gave it a deep-water berthage that it had previously lacked. A new swivel bridge was built just west of the Custom House in 1879 and named for the patriot Isaac Butt. It survived in that form, which allowed shipping to pass through it, until 1932, when the present solid structure replaced it. Right beside it, in 1891, was erected one of the city's true eyesores, the Loopline bridge, built to connect Westland Row and Amiens Street railway stations. More happily, Carlisle/O'Connell Bridge was widened in 1880 to the same width as Lower Sackville Street, leaving it literally as long as it is broad, one of the few truly square bridges in the world.

In the port itself, rail connections were eventually, after much delay, provided by the MGW and GSW companies to train sheds along the North Wall. The latter of these, known colloquially as the Southern Point, stood at the junction of the North Wall and East Wall Road. It was taken out of service as a goods terminal in the 1970s and converted to a concert venue, the Point, in the 1980s, undergoing a further transformation as the O_2 concert venue in recent years. The basic superstructure of the old Southern Point shed is still there, now topped by an incongruous and undistinguished architectural hat.

Any discussion of the port brings us back to the men who worked there and to the conditions in which they lived. The conditions were for the most part wretched and exploitative, with casual unskilled labour predominating. It left men with very little to offer the labour market other than their broad backs, placing them largely at the mercy of employers. Into this unequal world there now irrupted one of the great forces of nature in the city's history, Jim Larkin.

He had been born in Liverpool and left school at age 11 to work on the docks. In 1907, at the age of 31, he came to Ireland to organise the Belfast branch of the National Union of Dock Labourers. By August of that year he was in Dublin, organising the NUDL there. He mobilised the casual dockers and within the year had tripped off three strikes, much to the chagrin of the NUDL head office in Britain, which refused to finance the strikes. Larkin was never an easy colleague. Disgusted with the NUDL, he proceeded to form his own union, the Irish Transport & General Workers' (IT&GWU), in 1909. Over the next few years, his increasing militancy made him the sworn enemy of the Dublin employers. The climactic moment came in 1913, when William Martin Murphy, the dominant personality among the employers and proprietor of the Dublin United Tramway Company, locked out members of the IT&GWU who refused to sign a pledge to leave the union.

It was personal. Murphy and Larkin—each a big ego—detested each other. In response to the lockout, Larkin called a general strike at the end of August. Five days later, a heavily disguised Larkin entered the Imperial Hotel in Sackville Street, which was owned by Murphy, and began to harangue the crowd from a first-floor window. It was a audacious *coup de théâtre*. The DMP over-reacted to the excited crowd, whom they baton charged: over 300 members of the public were injured. 'Bloody Sunday' gave Larkin a moral victory. But the material victory eventually lay with the implacable Murphy. By early 1914, the men were effectively starved back to work. Every hand was against Larkin: the employers, naturally; the Catholic church, for the most part, ever suspicious of socialists; the mainstream nationalists, good bourgeois to a man; the British trades unions, who showed a most unfraternal attitude towards Larkin the longer the dispute went on.

Murphy and the employers had won, but historically it was a Pyrrhic victory. The poor of Dublin, living in conditions almost without parallel in the developed world, had a cause. Even if it was a losing cause for now, it had the making of a myth. Labour relations in the city were never the same again.

The social order of Victorian and Edwardian Dublin tolerated intolerable slums. It affected the outward piety and display of an ostentatiously Catholic city, yet tolerated a brothel area just behind Sackville Street which was one of the largest and most squalid in Europe: Joyce's Nighttown, known to Dubliners as Monto after its principal street, Montgomery Street (now Foley Street). But the old order was about to be swept away. A few months after the Lockout ended in defeat and Larkin had left for America, Europe's 99-year peace was broken. In faraway Sarajevo in Austrian Bosnia, Archduke Franz Ferdinand, heir to the Habsburg throne, was assassinated. By August, the Great War had begun.

11 CAPITAL OF INDEPENDENT IRELAND

The effect of the events of 1916–22 on the history of the city were transformative. By 1914, Parnell's successor John Redmond had secured the passage of a Home Rule Act in Westminster. It would have established a devolved Irish government in Dublin, autonomous in domestic affairs but still within the overall structure of the UK. The measure met adamantine opposition in those parts of Ulster with a Protestant majority, an opposition that proved politically irresistible. That, plus the outbreak of the war, caused the measure to be suspended for the duration.

By 1918, Europe was transformed and Ireland with it. A marginal faction of Irish republicans, the most radical and uncompromising of an uncompromising tradition, tripped off a revolt in arms against British rule in Ireland on Easter Monday 1916. Their purpose had been to strike while Britain was at war, on the time-honoured principle that 'England's difficulty was Ireland's opportunity'.

And so it happened. The rebels occupied a series of public buildings in Dublin and held them for nearly a week. The British government, as surprised as everyone else by this dramatic turn of events, had to divert some troops from the Western Front to combat the rising. It did not scruple to use artillery against rebel positions, of which the principal one—and the most symbolic—was Francis Johnston's General Post Office on Sackville Street. The result was the effective destruction of much of Lower Sackville Street, especially on the north side of the street.

Following the rebel surrender, 15 of the leaders were executed, thus giving the rising its martyrs. The momentum towards a more radical answer to the Irish nationalist question was now increased. Sinn Féin displaced Redmond's Parliamentary Party as the principal nationalist voice. A Treaty was eventually agreed with the British which gave the 26 counties independence outside the UK but not full republican status. This caused a split in republican ranks and a civil war, which the republican radicals opposed to the Treaty lost. However, in an eerie re-run of 1916, they too occupied public buildings in the city and were again routed by artillery, albeit this time fired by their own countrymen.

The principal loss to Dublin was twofold. The Four Courts was the principal republican garrison and it was reduced to a shell by an artillery attack. For historical reasons, it had housed the Public Record Office, which held invaluable manuscript sources on Irish history going back to the twelfth century. Before abandoning the building under artillery fire, the republicans set booby-trap bombs for the government forces, one of which exploded and reduced the PRO to ashes. The other loss was Upper O'Connell Street, as we must now call Sackville Street following its change of name. Lower O'Connell Street was still in ruins following 1916. Now the upper part of the street, especially on the northern side, was destroyed as government troops displaced the republican forces dug in there. Thus this side of the street was twice cursed, the lower end in 1916 and the upper end during the civil war.

The net effect was that the street had to be almost completely rebuilt. It was fortunate that the city archi-tects of the day, who oversaw the work, were both men of energy and taste. They were C.J. McCarthy and his successor, the wonderfully named Horace Tennyson O'Rourke. Between them, they gave Lower O'Connell Street, in particular, a pleasing and restrained architec-tural coherence. The Georgian classicism was gone for good and they resisted any temptation to restore it as pastiche. Instead they substituted a conservative commercial classicism typical of the first quarter of the new century. In Upper O'Connell Street, the restored Gresham Hotel (1927) was designed by the English architect Robert Atkinson. Its discreet neo-classicism, with just a hint of Egyptian decorative themes then in vogue, is particularly successful. Directly across from the Gresham, no. 42 is the last remaining authentically Georgian house in the entire street, an orphan remnant of the glory days.

———

From 1922, Dublin was a capital again. This time, however, it was no regional centre, but the capital city of an independent country. This meant many things, not least a considerable expansion of the bureaucratic infrastructure to reflect the transfer of administrative functions to the new regime. Finance and foreign affairs were the most obvious of these new functions, but the new state was also responsible for education, transport, policing and the legal system, defence, communications and local government. All these powers required the establishment and staffing of civil service departments. In a poor country, the securing of civil service positions, with their permanent and pensionable security of tenure, became the object of desire for many an ambitious provincial. In the eyes of Dubliners, Cork—now the second city of the new state—was especially fertile in supplying such people, one of whom was memorably described by Oliver St John Gogarty (Joyce's Buck Mulligan) as 'a country boy with hair in his ears and hair in his nose and a briefcase in his fist'.

This influx led in turn to further suburban expansion, with areas being developed on both sides of the river.

The inter-war period saw significant developments in this regard. It also saw the first serious attempts at major slum-clearance projects, in a series of initiatives that did great credit to the governments of independent Ireland, and stood them in a very positive contrast with the old British regime. They were helped by an ideological acceptance of publicly funded housing schemes that had not existed in Victorian days. The result contrasted with earlier efforts to address the problem of the tenements which had been worthy but feeble.

The late nineteenth century had seen some successful attempts at private philanthropic initiative to relieve the situation. The establishment of the Dublin Artisans' Dwelling Company in 1876 was one such. It was established by members of the Dublin Sanitary Association, who leased sites from the Corporation that the latter had already acquired and cleared. Their most successful scheme was just off the Coombe in the Liberties, where the sturdy cottages they built still stand in a planned environment that is pleasing to the eye. However, as the company's name suggests, the schemes of the DADC were not aimed at the indigent poor, but at skilled tradesmen and their families. References were required before a tenant could take possession and regular employment in a steady job was a prerequisite. The company was run as a commercial entity, not as a charity, and was designed to yield a return to its investors. As for the Corporation, the cost of acquiring the Coombe site originally and then clearing it was not recouped by the paltry sum for which it leased it to the

DADC, so that it served less as a precedent than as a warning.

The other major Victorian initiative had been the Guinness Trust, established in 1890 by Sir Arthur Edward Guinness, who donated £50,000 in trust to alleviate bad housing conditions in the city. This mutated into the Iveagh Trust in 1903. It cleared the area between St Patrick's Cathedral and Werburgh Street, one notorious even by Dublin standards, created St Patrick's Park beside the cathedral and constructed the imposing red-brick apartment buildings in Bull Alley Street and environs.

These initiatives, while successful in themselves, left the greater part of the problem untouched. It was not until the new state took a direct hand in the matter in the 1920s and 1930s that real progress started to be made. The beautifully laid-out Marino estate on the north side was a product of the 1920s. On the south side, Crumlin, bigger than Marino and less successful visually and architecturally, was none the less a blessing for families that had hitherto faced nothing other than exorbitant rents in squalid city-centre tenements. Nearby, Drimnagh was also developed as a public housing estate in a similar fashion, as were Cabra and Finglas on the north side. This all meant the commitment of public funds on a lavish scale, an achievement all the more meritorious for the fact that the state was poor.

The effect was that the twentieth century and an independent government managed to resolve the biggest social problem that had defeated the nineteenth-century British administration. Other forces helped, not least Catholic lay organisations like the Legion of Mary, whose Marian ardour was offended by the widespread prostitution in the city and which campaigned success-fully to close the Monto town. They saw the overcrowded slums as a breeding ground for vice: a by-product of their zeal was the increased political pressure which the Catholic Church—by now in a position of uncontested moral authority in the country—could bring to bear on government.

The slum clearance schemes reinforced an historic pattern by emphasising that the west of the city was mainly for the poorer classes and the east for the relatively well-to-do. The majority of the new slum clearance public housing estates were in the west, logically enough, since that was where land was most readily available. East was the sea, north was the airport, south were the mountains: the west was easiest. But it reinforced a stark east–west divide that had been growing for 200 years and that now represented the real social demarcation in city life. Much humour is expended on north side–south side jokes, and the differences they invoke have psychological reality, but the east–west divide is more potent sociologically.

———

The decades from independence to the end of the 1950s are generally regarded as a time of stagnation. One historian titled his book on the period *Preventing the Future,* with an even more telling subtitle: *Why Ireland was So Poor for So Long.* Dublin was no exception to the general rule. Emigration—a constant in Irish life since the Famine—continued unabated and reached frightening proportions in the 1950s. The city had been bypassed by the Industrial Revolution and remained largely a commercial city with no heavy industry and very few large enterprises, of which Guinness remained the most famous.

Culturally, the new state enjoyed the prestige of seeing two Dublin natives, Yeats and Shaw, receive the Nobel Prize for Literature in the 1920s, and the opening of the Gate Theatre in 1928 brought international drama, presented to the highest professional standards, to the city for the first time. Alas, it was a less happy time at the Abbey. A second major riot greeted Sean O'Casey's *The Plough and the Stars* in 1926, his play set during the rising 10 years earlier. That, plus the Abbey's rejection of his next offering, *The Silver Tassie,* drove O'Casey into embittered exile in England. The theatre then fell under the management of Ernest Blythe, a narrow-minded ex-politician and Irish-language enthusiast, in whose dead hand it atrophied for a generation.

It was a wretched time for writers given the state's hostile indifference to literature. This was best (or worst) expressed in the fit of rural peasant piety that was the Censorship of Publications Act 1929, which made Ireland a laughing-stock by banning just about every modern novelist of any literary stature. None the less,

the city's literary tradition continued to flourish, albeit
in difficult circumstances. Even the vast shadow of Yeats,
who lived until 1939, could not prevent the emergence of
a younger generation of poets, of whom Patrick
Kavanagh was the most gifted. His *The Great Hunger* is
the most compelling poetic work to emerge from
Ireland towards the mid-century. His friend Brian
O'Nolan/Flann O'Brien/Myles na Gopaleen produced
two novels of genius, *At Swim-Two-Birds* (1939) and *The
Third Policeman* (1941/1967), but the rejection of the
latter as a result of wartime restrictions disturbed his
development as a novelist: the book was eventually
published posthumously. In his Myles persona, he
developed into what many regarded as the funniest
newspaper columnist in the world. His 'Cruiskeen Lawn'
column in the *Irish Times* was manically exuberant, and
contributed significantly to the gradual revival of that
newspaper. But alcoholism dulled his talent and he
never fulfilled his early promise as a novelist, two late
works being feeble by comparison with his brilliant
beginning.

No discussion of literature in twentieth-century
Dublin can ignore James Joyce's *Ulysses*, published in
the year the new state was founded, 1922. Although Joyce
had left Dublin in 1904—the year in which the novel is
set—and had only returned for two brief visits in 1909
and 1912, he writes about the city with an intimacy that
has no parallel in literature. Not even Dickens' London
feels as real as Joyce's Dublin: the kaleidoscope of urban
characters; the uncanny ear for the nuances of Dublin

speech and diction; the evocation of the city's atmosphere and personality by a manipulation of language that is masterly and complete. Joyce did not like his native city, his 'centre of paralysis', but he presented it with a breathtaking fidelity. Even at the remove of time since composition and publication, anyone with close knowledge of the city will recognise it from the pages of this masterpiece.

———

The Eucharistic Congress of 1932 was the great set-piece of the new Catholic ascendancy. A papal legate came from Rome; John McCormack sang for the million-strong congregation at a Mass in the Phoenix Park. A special altar was erected on O'Connell Bridge. All in all, it was an unambiguous statement of Catholic power.

That power was consolidated from 1940 by one of the most remarkable men ever to occupy the position of Archbishop of Dublin, John Charles McQuaid. A rigorist and an ascetic of narrow but acute intelligence, he oversaw a huge expansion of the institutional church in the city. Between 1948 and 1965, he built 34 new churches and 67 secondary schools to serve the expanding suburbs. He established a number of social agencies to give the church a key voice in areas of family support where he had a pathological suspicion of the state. He was instrumental in procuring the dismissal of a left-wing maverick Minister for Health whose Mother and Child Scheme would have provided free medical care for mothers and their children under 16 years of age. This was offensive to McQuaid's belief that the state should not usurp (as he saw it) the proper responsibility of the family in such matters, although he clearly had the Church in mind as well. In fact, the archbishop had a distinctly nineteenth-century view of social provision and the role of the state; in many respects he was still fighting the French Revolution.

But McQuaid's day was passing. The dismal 1950s, a time of bleak social and economic stagnation and of terrifying levels of emigration, were about to yield to the sixties, when Ireland enjoyed its first period of real economic expansion since the Famine, along with novelties like television, supermarkets and the first shoots of secularism. The high-water mark of Catholic power was past, although few recognised this at the time. The 1960s were to further alter the face of the Irish capital. After generations of stagnation, there were going to be some changes made.

12 | DUBLIN SINCE THE 1960s

The boom of the 1960s was quite remarkable given the economic history of Ireland since the Famine. It was soon forgotten, as the slump of the 1970s and the locust years that followed seemed to swallow its gains. But while it lasted it produced genuine growth and an increase in household wealth, an end to emigration, the first questioning of the moral monopoly of the Catholic Church and an impulse towards modernity. It marked the generational change from the revolutionary to the post-revolutionary. The men who made the revolution were symbolised by Eamon de Valera (1882–1975), who had only stepped down as Taoiseach in 1959 and then assumed the Presidency. The new generation were nearly all born after the foundation of the state, the most glamorous and talented of them being Charles Haughey (1925–2006).

Unlike their stuffy and severe seniors, the new generation were fun. They were making a wave of prosperity and surfing it. Unfortunately, the whiff of corruption was present from the start, especially where Haughey was concerned. He lived an extravagant, aristocratic lifestyle way beyond his visible means. His country house in north Co. Dublin had been built for none other than John Beresford—the onlie begetter of the Custom House—and designed by Gandon. Haughey may not have initiated the growing connection between Fianna Fáil, the almost-permanent government party, and the construction industry, but he symbolised it. From the mid-sixties, FF became the builders' party. And Haughey became the builders' kept man, as was eventually discovered in the 1990s when the sources of his 'wealth' eventually came to light.

Builders are there to build, and economic booms give them every incentive to do so. The 1960s were no exception. The builders and speculators were for the most part from rural backgrounds—a hugely disproportionate number from the west of Ireland—and tended to be FF supporters both by inclination and material interest. That meant no love or empathy for Georgian architecture. There was no doubting the decay in what was left of the slums. In 1963, in Bolton Street, a Georgian tenement collapsed in the small hours of the morning, killing two elderly occupants. In Fenian Street, near Merrion Square, another house collapse 10 days later killed two little girls on their way to a shop. It would have required a culture of heroic restoration to revive streets like these. But very few were interested in restoration.

So the decayed Georgian tenement houses were gradually replaced by hideous public-authority flats, while the houses in the better areas of the city—the south-east quadrant for the most part—were targeted for redevelopment. In these areas, the problem was shabby-genteel decline rather than dereliction, but these were places in which developers could turn a profit.

Two developments must stand for the 1960s barbarism, Fitzwilliam Street and Hume Street. In 1964, the state-owned Electricity Supply Board got planning permission to demolish nos 13–28 Lower Fitzwilliam Street, which it owned and wished to replace with a modern office block. The demolition was completed the following year and the office block was duly built and fully opened in 1970. The best that can be said of it is that it could have been worse. It is undistinguished, but at least it maintained the horizontal roof line of what it replaced, so that its effect on what had been the city's longest continuous Georgian vista—from Holles Street hospital to Leeson Street—was less than it otherwise might have been. But it was and still is the wrong building in the wrong place.

Hume Street was slightly different, although the issue was the same. The two houses in question, on the corner of Hume Street and St Stephen's Green, were owned by the state and sold to a developer. Coming in the wake of the Fitzwilliam Street fiasco, it led to an occupation of the site by protesters before it was eventually redeveloped in a deeply unsuccessful and insensitive Georgian pastiche. The protest was evidence of a changing sensibility as the decade turned into the 1970s, albeit a minority sensibility still. Some of the protesters were architectural students; a few years earlier, at the time of the ESB controversy, architectural students voiced their support for the development, on the shallow but understandable basis that they did not want Dublin to become a museum city. Something had shifted in the intervening years.

The two oil crises of the 1970s and spectacular economic mismanagement by government brought the boom to a shuddering end. From the mid-1970s to the early 1990s, it seemed that the bad old days were back again: the best and the brightest were emigrating in droves. The building boom slowed accordingly, although it was the mid-1980s before it really hit the buffers, with the collapse of the property empire of Patrick Gallagher, heir to a family business that had always been very close to Charles Haughey. A month before the banks called in the receiver to the Gallagher empire, Patrick had valued his assets at £60m. A year later, their estimated realisable value was down to £26m. He was not alone. The building craze was over for the moment.

There are few major buildings from the 25 years following 1960, especially on sensitive sites, that are unqualified successes. Some, such as the hideous Liberty Hall beside the Custom House, are a blot on the landscape. The same can be said for Apollo House and Hawkins House in Poolbeg Street, just on the other side of Butt Bridge. To be fair, buildings such as the Central Bank in Dame Street and the headquarters of the Bank of Ireland in Baggot Street have their champions, with some justice. But in general, it was a dismal time for architecture. Dublin—in its mania to appear modern (and turn a buck)—may be said to have hitched a ride on the international style at a time when that style was at a low ebb.

Meanwhile the relentless suburban sprawl went on as the population grew. The demand was not for apartments or any other form of high-density accommodation, but for suburban semi-detached houses with gardens fore and aft. This meant a huge city footprint, as land was acquired for building way out into what had previously been the countryside. This process would falter in the 1980s without ever quite stopping and then roar back to life with a vengeance in the Celtic Tiger years from the mid-1990s.

This led to two consequences worth noting, among many. First, it became a licence to print money for holders of agricultural land who could get it rezoned for building. The landowners thus had a common interest with the developers: they wanted to sell, the developers wanted to buy. The snag was getting the rezoning through. This was the responsibility of the City Council, many of whose members were induced through bribery to 'do the right thing'. A cottage industry grew up whereby councillors took the dosh and voted the re-zoning, often against the anguished advice of city planners.

There was deep corruption in the planning process for many years. Bribery was the least of it. The key was a network of builders and politicians who scratched each others' backs. One cabinet minister had an expensive house built for him by builders to whom he was notoriously close and for whom he was believed to have facilitated rezonings. The revelations that have emerged in a series of tribunals lasting many years are probably no more than the tip of the iceberg. There was simply too much money to be made—and quickly. It was irresistible. But the urban fabric has been the victim of this well-connected private avarice.

The second consequence of low-density suburban sprawl was the near-impossibility of running an efficient public transport system to service it. All integrated systems depend on densities far higher than anything Dublin was developing. On top of that, transport policy for the city remained shambolic and chaotic. The trams were abandoned way back in 1949, since when the buses have been the workhorses of the system. The coastal suburban railway—part of the Belfast main line on the north side and the Wexford main line on the south— was electrified in the 1980s and rebranded as the DART (Dublin Area Rapid Transit). It is of course no such thing; it is just a single line and, while excellent in itself, links to no other similar line. There is an outer suburban rail system (Arrow) to serve the dormitory towns that exploded in the Celtic Tiger years. And there is the Luas—a modernised tram system, all very nice and well patronised—but it comprises a mere two lines with no interchange between them. To top it all, there is no integrated ticketing between rail, bus and tram systems.

This is a massive political failure over many years. The result is that the modern city is excessively car dependent. Very sensibly, an orbital motorway, the M50, was developed from the late 1980s onwards. It was recommended that it be built with three lanes each way but government cheeseparing allowed only two, an economy soon shown to be short-sighted. Before long, the M50 was notorious for traffic congestion. The state then compounded its folly by granting planning permissions to property interests to develop shopping centres and other retail and business parks along the route of the motorway, thus vitiating its function. Instead of being a relief road, it is an access road.

An example of what intelligent planning can achieve is shown in the Temple Bar area, just south of the river. Neglected for years, much of it was owned by CIÉ, the national transport company, which intended to make it the city's principal transport hub. While waiting to complete its property portfolio in fulfilment of this scheme, it let its existing properties at low rents. This attracted artists and quirky shops to the area. Out of this, an idea was born that the transport plan might be aborted and the area turned into a cultural quarter. This obviously required political muscle, and to his eternal credit it was forthcoming from Charles Haughey, Taoiseach from 1987 to 1992. This fascinating, malevolent, corrupt and charming man established a not-for-profit company to oversee the development of the area.

It has been an almost unqualified success. There is a mixture of residential property, retail, restaurants, pubs (too many), theatres, studios and, most of all, an air of energy and even style. It is a model for what could be done elsewhere with greater political imagination and will.

Another Haughey initiative was the International Financial Services Centre on the north quays, which prompted a wholesale redevelopment of the quays on both sides of the river from Talbot Memorial Bridge to the East Link. The IFSC drew subsidiaries of major international finance houses to Dublin to participate in the long financial boom that ended only in the crash of 2008. It helped that the IFSC acquired a reputation for slack regulation, even by the standards of an international financial system where light regulation was the prevailing norm. During the boom, the culture of the IFSC was either denied or (more plausibly) explained by saying that Ireland was coming from a long way back and needed to buy some competitive advantage. It was great while it lasted; it looks less pretty now.

However, the new buildings at the IFSC are outstandingly successful and are a genuine addition to the city's furniture. A whole residential area, suitably high-density, has grown up right behind it, although at its margins it touches on one of the poorest subsisting areas of old Dublin around Sheriff Street. As in the eighteenth century, new wealth and old poverty can be cheek by jowl. Along the river front, a series of handsome if rather unambitious buildings have greatly improved what had been a derelict area. The new National Conference Centre, a dramatic exception to the prevailing caution, is the stand-out building that the area needs.

——

Culturally, the city has been enriched since the 1960s. The opening of the National Concert Hall in the 1980s in Earlsfort Terrace, on the site of UCD's old Aula Max, filled a gap of long standing. UCD had abandoned the Terrace for suburban Belfield 10 years earlier. The removal of a major university from the city centre may have been practical but was culturally dubious. Trinity reclaimed its status as a central city institution, partly as a result of its rival's departure to the suburbs, and partly because a ban on Catholic students studying there was lifted in the 1970s. The first major exhibition of international art in the modern idiom took place in 1967 under the rubric ROSC. Since then, the development of the new Royal Hibernian Gallery in Ely Place and of the Irish Museum of Modern Art in the Royal Hospital Kilmainham have enriched the city's life. The National Museum of Ireland has expanded its holdings and premises under the energetic direction of Dr Patrick Wallace. The Chester Beatty Library, containing the treasures of a private collector, was moved into custom-built premises in Dublin Castle in the 1990s. It holds an exceptional collection of Islamic and Asian manuscripts and artefacts, and is deservedly one of the major tourist attractions in the city.

It could be argued that Croke Park, the headquarters of the Gaelic Athletic Association on the north side, is the single most impressive structure put up in the city in living memory. It is the fourth-largest sports stadium in Europe by capacity and is an architectural and design triumph.

———

The city retains its distinct personality. It is not for nothing that Joyce's *Ulysses* still resonates. There is new-money glitter and shabby gentility side by side. There is still downright poverty among large numbers of people untouched or little touched by the boom. Even many of those better off are heavily indebted as a result of borrowing against inflating property values that have now started to tumble again, leaving Ireland with the unenviable record of having the highest rate of personal debt to income in the developed world. The city is vastly more self-assured than it was at the start of the 1960s but, as always, there are anxieties and fears for the future. The collapse in property values has caught many people out. Getting around is an increasing problem given the dysfunctional state of public transport. But the city at its best still retains its peculiar charm: the salty, slightly malicious wit; the old pubs; the view along Merrion Square north to the Pepper Canister Church.

SELECT BIBLIOGRAPHY

— Bennett, Douglas, *Encyclopaedia of Dublin*, Dublin: Gill & Macmillan 1994

— Boran, Pat, *A Short History of Dublin*, Cork: Mercier Press 2000

— Boylan, Henry, *A Dictionary of Irish Biography*, 3rd ed., Dublin: Gill & Macmillan 1998

— Brady, Joseph & Simms, Anngret, eds, *Dublin Through Space and Time*, Dublin: Four Courts Press 2001

— Clarke, H.B., ed., *Medieval Dublin: the making of a metropolis*, Dublin: Irish Academic Press 1990

— Clarke, H.B., ed., *Medieval Dublin: the living city*, Dublin: Irish Academic Press 1990

— Clarke, Howard B., ed., *Irish Cities*, Cork: Mercier Press 1995

— Clear, Catriona, *Social Change and Everyday Life in Ireland 1850–1922*, Manchester: MUP 2007

— Connolly, S.J., *Contested Island: Ireland 1460–1630*, Oxford: OUP 2007

— Connolly, S.J., ed., *The Oxford Companion to Irish History*, Oxford: OUP 1998

— Craig, Maurice, *Dublin 1660–1860*, Dublin: Allen Figgis 1969

— Daly, Mary E., *Dublin, The Deposed Capital: a social and economic history 1860–1914*, Cork: Cork UP 1984

— De Courcy, J.W., *The Liffey in Dublin*, Dublin: Gill & Macmillan 1996

— Duffy, Sean et al., *Atlas of Irish History*, Dublin: Gill & Macmillan 1997

— Fagan, Patrick, *The Second City: portrait of Dublin 1700–1760*, Dublin: Branar 1986

— Ferriter, Diarmaid, *The Transformation of Ireland 1900–2000*, London: Profile 2004

— Ferriter, Diarmaid, *Occasions of Sin: sex & society in modern Ireland*, London: Profile 2009

— Gilligan, H.A., *A History of the Port of Dublin*, Dublin: Gill & Macmillan 1988

— Kearns, Kevin C., *Dublin Tenement Life: an oral history*, Dublin: Gill & Macmillan 1994
— Kilfeather, Siobhán, *Dublin: a cultural and literary history*, Dublin: Liffey Press 2005
— Lydon, James, *The Making of Ireland: from ancient times to the present*, London: Routledge 1998
— McDonald, Frank, *The Destruction of Dublin*, Dublin: Gill & Macmillan 1985
— McGee, Owen, *The IRB: the Irish Republican Brotherhood from the Land League to Sinn Féin*, Dublin: Four Courts Press 2005
— Maxwell, Constantia, *Dublin Under the Georges*, London: Harrap 1946
— Milne, Kenneth, ed., *Christ Church Cathedral: a history*, Dublin: Four Courts Press 2000
— O'Brien, Joseph V., *Dear Dirty Dublin: a city in distress 1899–1916*, London: University of California Press 1982
— O'Donnell, E.E., *The Annals of Dublin's Fair City*, Dublin: Wolfhound Press 1987
— Ó Gráda, Cormac, *Ireland: a new economic history 1789–1939*, Oxford: Clarendon Press 1994
— Ó Siochrú, Micheál, *God's Executioner: Oliver Cromwell and the conquest of Ireland*, London: Faber & Faber 2008
— Pearson, Peter, *The Heart of Dublin: resurgence of an historic city*, Dublin: O'Brien Press 2000
— Townshend, Charles, *Easter 1916: the Irish rebellion*, London: Allen Lane 2005
— Welch, Robert, ed., *The Oxford Companion to Irish Literature*, Oxford: OUP 1996
— Wills, Claire, *That Neutral Island: a cultural history of Ireland during the Second World War*, London: Faber & Faber 2007
— Yeates, Padraig, *Lockout: Dublin 1913*, Dublin: Gill & Macmillan 2000

INDEX